DEAR MS. WHOLENESS

DEAR MS. WHOLENESS

SHAVON CARTER

PURPOSED PUBLISHING COMPANY
BOWIE, MD

Dear Ms. Wholeness

ISBN 978-0-692-78722-9

Purposed Publishing Company
1019 Fallcrest Ct.
Bowie, MD 20721

Cover design by Stephen Fortune
Editing by Monica Brown
Editing and Proofreading by Final Touch Proofreading & Editing, LLC
Layout and Design by MonkeyMind Studios, LLC

Printed in the United States of America

To my Heavenly Father: Thank you for every trial I faced that equipped me to write this book. Thank you for carrying me through it all. Without you, I am nothing.

Contents

Preface

"Honey, I'm home!" I announced happily as I walked in the door on October 6, 2012—the day my life changed forever.

It was a little after ten p.m., and I had just come from a birthday dinner for my godmother, who had turned fifty-eight. My two god-sisters and I had taken her out to celebrate. Prior to leaving for the dinner, my husband and I had watched television and enjoyed a passionate, impromptu lovemaking session. High on cloud nine, I got dressed and met one of my god-sisters outside so we could ride together. Just before we left, my husband came out, chatted with us for a while, and then went back in the house. I had a wonderful evening celebrating my godmother.

Eager to tell him all about our time together and the good food, I was disappointed when I didn't hear a response to my greeting. But I figured he was in the office or the bathroom and just didn't hear me. I walked down the hallway and checked both rooms, but he wasn't there. "Maybe he's out in the car," I thought to myself. He would often go to the car to meditate and have some quiet time since our two-bedroom condo with a loft didn't offer much space for alone time. Although I had just come from the parking lot, I hadn't paid attention to our ten-year-old Nissan Altima parked outside to notice whether he had been sitting in it. Now, I peeked through the wooden blinds toward the parking lot, but our car was empty. My mind began to wander, so I sent him a text message asking where he was. "Perhaps one of his friends came to pick him up," I reasoned.

Feeling confident that he would respond shortly as he always did, I turned on the TV show *Iyanla, Fix My Life.* My friend had messaged me about an episode on backstabbing friends. I watched as it depicted six friends who had started a blog site together to show that black women could get along, but instead, their relationships had fallen apart and they needed Iyanla to help them mend things. The show reminded me of two of my closest girlfriends and the organization with a similar mission that we had been talking about starting.

Midway through the show, I noticed that my husband hadn't responded to my text message, so I called him. No answer. "Hmm, that's strange," I thought. But shortly after hanging up, I received an odd text message from him: "I give up. You deserve better, so much better."

"What the hell?" I said aloud. "I deserve *you!* Stop tripping. We're in this together. Where are you? Where are you, Jeff?" He had been feeling down lately, especially this week after being notified that he hadn't gotten the job he'd been hoping for.

It had been tough for both of us since he had gotten laid off from his job in February, 2011. But I believed that this was the season God had us in right now and that in due time, things would get better. Seeing that my husband still hadn't responded to my earlier messages, I fired back, "So you're just ignoring me right now? Really?!" I sat on the couch confused about what was going on. What was he talking about? Where was he?

Then something prompted me to go to our bedroom and look around. I glanced at the clear three-drawer storage bin where his under-wear, socks, and t-shirts usually were—it was empty. I walked to our closet and slid open the side of the mirrored door where his clothes hung—all his clothes and shoes were gone. Shocked, I walked to our office and looked in the closet where he stored more clothes, only to find it empty. He was gone, and he had taken everything with him.

I headed back to the living room and sat down in a daze. Again I text-messaged him: "Wow . . . So you left me? Wow . . . You packed all your stuff and left me . . . Wow."

After I pressed Send, every emotion that was in me came rushing out like a flood. I cried uncontrollably, struggling to catch my breath. Not knowing what to do, I sent a text to my two closest friends, Lisa and Tasha. Immediately, they both replied that they were on their way over. Ironically, the scene from Iyanla's show had just come on when the friends hovered around each other to console the one friend who had to come to grips with her husband's terminal illness. Little did I know that a similar situation was about to take place in my home.

As I sat waiting for my friends to arrive, my husband texted back. "I'm lost. Lost hope. Lost faith. Losing the war, lost the battle." Clearly, he was depressed, and I was worried that he would do something to hurt himself, so I responded, "Are you headed to Miami? I need to know that you're safe. I need to know that you're not gonna do nothing crazy to yourself." He said he didn't know. Although my heart had just sunk with the realization that he had left, I put my feelings aside to make sure he was okay. For many years I had denied my own feelings to please a guy, and this time was no exception.

Miami is where he is originally from, and he often went back to visit on the weekends to pursue a business venture, so I had a feeling he was headed there. I feared he was delusional and might have suicidal thoughts, so I sent him another text: "Promise me you won't do anything to harm yourself."

He replied, "I promise."

By this time, my friend Lisa had arrived. She walked in, immediately gave me a big hug, and told me she had called our other close friend, Dana, to come over too. We sat on the couch and I told her what had happened. She was just as stunned as I was. There were so many unanswered questions: Why did he leave? Where was he going? How was he getting there? Was our marriage over? There was so much I didn't understand, and soon Dana and Tasha were also there to comfort me. They just sat and listened as I rambled, vented, and shed a few tears. In an attempt to piece the facts of the situation together, I checked our bank account to see what activity had occurred. I saw that Jeff had rented a car with our credit card and taken $200 out of our savings account. There was a gas purchase, so, using the name of the gas station, we performed an Internet search to see where it was located. He was in South Carolina. Since that state was at least five hours away from us in Maryland, we concluded that he had left shortly after I left for my dinner. This move was premeditated.

My friends sat with me for a couple of hours until they could see that I was calm. Before they left, we all stood in a circle and they prayed for Jeff and me. I felt so blessed to have such loving and caring friends. They didn't judge, bash, or offer their opinion. Their assignment was to make sure I was okay, and I appreciated their support. After our prayer, I walked them to the door, then went back and sat on the couch.

I picked up the phone and texted Jeff: "Is our marriage over? I still love you and I plan to stick by you even in this. I'm not giving up on you. You're my husband and I vow to be with you forever. For better or for worse, for richer or for poorer, in sickness and in health, till death do us part. We will get through this. I love you, Jeff. I don't want anyone else but you. You're my husband. You are worthy of love."

Within moments, he responded, "I love you, Shavon, and you are an awesome wife."

But if that was the case, how did we end up here? With my mind racing, I decided to reach out to two of Jeff's friends to let them know what had happened in hopes that they would pray and reach out to him. His mind was in disarray, so I figured he needed someone to talk some sense into him. Then, feeling tired and drained and noticing that it was almost four a.m., I managed to move from the sofa to the bed and fell off to sleep for a little while. However, I couldn't rest because I was still concerned about my husband.

I woke up around seven and called and messaged him to see where he was. Around eight, he responded by text that he had made it to Orlando. He said his two friends had also called and messaged him—had I called them? I told him yes, I had contacted them because I was worried about him. I could tell by his response that he was annoyed. He said he didn't want anyone to know what had happened, not even those who loved and cared about him. In an effort to get him to talk more, I tried to be compassionate and caring and said, "Bless your heart. You're just driving and you don't know what to do." He responded with emoticons of sad crying faces. I continued, "You're probably feeling confused, ashamed, and so many other emotions. You're headed in the direction of the place that brings you comfort, which is home. I wish I had the answer. I wish I could just make it all better."

"I know," he said.

"My heart aches for you," I said. "Do you think you will ever come back here?"

"Mine aches for me too," he replied. By this time he was about two hours away from Miami. I thanked him for continuing to text me back because it helped to relieve some of my worry. I continued trying to make small talk by telling him about the restaurant we had gone to the night before and how good the food was. I told him we would have to go there once he got back. It was obvious I was in denial about him leaving and not coming back, but I continued to talk about things we could do together. I even told him that if I went back to Italy, I wanted to buy him a suit this time because I knew he really wanted one from there. In October 2011, my job had flown me to Italy for three weeks for a project, so I had paid for Jeff to fly over too, as a birthday gift, so we could enjoy it together. While there, he had wanted to get an Italian suit, but we didn't have the extra money for shopping. There was talk at work about my team going back there for some follow-up work, and this time I would make sure I got him a suit. My mind continued sorting through thoughts to find understanding, but nothing made sense.

In light of all that, it might seem odd, but I now look back and see that the night my husband left was the moment my healing journey began. I've spoken to many women who've gone through painful experiences and struggled to find peace. The question they often ask is "How do I get through this and heal?"

I wrote this book as a personal letter to every woman who has ever wondered "How?" I refer to you, dear sister, as Ms. Wholeness because I believe that you are complete and lack nothing, even if it feels like your life is broken into a million pieces. In this book I vulnerably and transparently share my "How" to serve as a gateway for your healing and wholeness. Consider me your midwife standing beside you, holding your hand, helping you give birth to a new you. It may be painful as you read my story and reflect on your own experiences. But in the midst of those times I will be gently encouraging you to push through the pain in service of your healing.

Let's begin this journey of healing that will lead to peace, love, joy, and freedom to walk in who you are . . . Ms. Wholeness.

One
How Did I Get Here?

I've been told I was the cutest little baby. I didn't give my mom much trouble. She was young—only seventeen—when she had me. My mom would buy me cute little clothes and dress me up. All the people in the neighborhood where we lived in Jacksonville, Florida, wanted to babysit me, but my mom and grandma kept me close and didn't allow it. I was their pride and joy. I'm not sure if my dad felt the same way because he wasn't really around. In fact, I only remember seeing one picture of him holding me while my mom sat next to him and smiled. He was young also—nineteen—and often running the streets and getting in trouble with the law. I guess he had his own set of issues to work through. My mom said she sometimes took me to see him while he was in jail, until one day I asked her why Dad couldn't come home with us. After that, she stopped taking me.

Until I was ten years old, I was raised by my mom and grand-mother. Despite her age, my mom was very wise and attentive to my needs. When I was around two, she heard me singing a TV commercial. She immediately turned off the television and said if I could remember the words to the commercial, I could learn my ABCs. From then on, she instilled in me the importance of learning and doing well in school.

In preschool, I was a tiny thing, but I had a head full of thick hair that my mom used to style so nicely. I remember one year being the queen of my preschool because I had sold the most for our school fund-raiser. A picture was taken of me standing on stage wearing a long cream dress that covered my feet, a red cloak around my tiny little shoulders, and a tiara on my head. I was being escorted by the little boy who had been named king for the fundraiser. I guess you can say that he was my very first boyfriend—or at least that's what I thought! Neither of us knew anything about being boyfriend and girlfriend, but somehow he knew that the boy was supposed to like and care for the girl, so that's what he did. After preschool, it was time for me to go to school with the big kids, so I graduated and went on to first grade.

My memories of early childhood are full of joy and happiness. I remember swinging on swing sets, riding my bike with training wheels, and getting dolls and toys for Christmas. On my first day of school, my mom dressed me in a cute little yellow dress with a rainbow-colored belt and shoes to match. My hair was neatly pulled back in pigtails, and I looked like a little woman! Like my mom and grandmother, I was always smiling and posing for the camera. I smiled even when my teeth started to come out and I was missing two in the front. My first-grade school pictures show me with a cute little blue sailor dress, four pigtails, lacy socks, and matching shoes.

I was a "mommy's girl," so I slept in her bed for a long time; it made me feel safe. My grandmother was the matriarch of the family and made sure I went to church every Sunday and was involved in all the church youth activities and events. By the time I reached fourth grade, I had gotten a little taller and my hair hung almost to my shoulders. I graduated from the pigtails and got a relaxer put in my hair, and my mom combed it to the side and gave me a bang. One of the girls in my class and I used to compete to see whose ponytail was the longest—oh, the silly things we did in elementary school! It didn't matter, though. I felt cute and loved by my mom and grandma, so all was well in my life. Those were some good times, Ms. Wholeness, but little did I know that things were about to change.

By the time I reached fifth grade, the Jheri curl was the popular hairstyle, and my mom let me get one. The relaxers I was getting had damaged my hair, so I had to get it cut off, and I figured a Jheri curl was the next-best thing. Around that same time I had to get glasses. They had big red frames, and the lenses were tinted so they turned into sunglasses in the sun. They actually overpowered my small face. I had gotten a little taller by then, but I was still short and skinny. At eleven, it seemed like the cute little girl with the ponytail and bright smile had suddenly turned into an ugly duckling.

Changes were also happening in my family. My mom had met a man on the night of my tenth birthday party, when she went out after my friends and I fell asleep. They had gotten engaged shortly after that, and in June of the following year, they were married.

The wedding was beautiful. The colors were peach and teal green, which seemed to blend so nicely. I wore a beautiful peach dress and stood at the front as a junior bridesmaid, alongside the rest of the wedding party. My mom looked beautiful, but I remember being sad, too. I had gotten used to life with just the two of us (and my grandma). Mom and I did everything together, so I wasn't looking forward to sharing her with someone else. Nevertheless, after the wedding, she and I moved out of my grandmother's house into an apartment with my new stepfather.

My initial memories of our transition are a blur. I don't remember how I felt about him or what kind of relationship we had at first, so I assume that, in the beginning, things were okay. We lived in the apartment for a short time and then moved into the house my stepfather had grown up in. It is in this house that the painful memories begin.

I was now in sixth grade at a school about a mile down the street. Oh, Ms. Wholeness, I was such a nerd, taking gifted classes and making the honor roll! I loved to read and write, so I was excited when my sixth-grade teacher introduced us to creative writing. And so I learned the art of expressing myself with a pen.

Although I did well in the classroom, I didn't fare too well socially. If I had to pinpoint the start of my self-esteem issues, it would be during this time. It all started when a boy was interested in me and I liked him, too. He wasn't part of the gifted program, so his classroom was in a different hallway than mine. He was in a class with a group of girls, including one he was in a relationship with before me. When the news got out that he and I were together, she and the other girls in his class were not very happy. Later I found out that his ex-girlfriend was jealous of me, not only because I was with him, but because I was smart and wore cute clothes. My mom and I were shopping buddies, so every Friday she would buy me a new outfit to wear to school. This boy's ex started threatening me and talking about all the bad things she was going to do to me. Ms. Wholeness, I was terrified because I had never gotten into a fight in my life, not even an altercation. I didn't know what to do! I was still the skinny little girl with the big glasses and the Jheri curl who did well in class and loved to learn. But every time I saw his ex and her friends, I became so fearful, not knowing what they might do to me.

Well, one day, I was in line with my class getting ready to go outside for recess. As we headed outside, the girl's class was coming in. As she walked by, she punched me really hard—right in my face! I was so embarrassed because this was a busy part of the day; a lot of kids had witnessed this assault. Feeling defenseless, I just kept walking as if it had never happened. One of my classmates, a close friend of mine, found out what had happened and attempted to defend me by fighting the girl who had punched me. Although I appreciated her taking up for me, her actions couldn't undo the damage done. I was traumatized, and it became difficult for me to trust other females.

After that incident, my boyfriend and I broke up, and I became the laughingstock of the school. Many of the kids looked for any reason to laugh at and pick on me. For instance, one day when I wore a little pink skirt set to school, the boy I had recently broken up with said he thought I looked like a sheep and gave me the nickname "Baaaa." That name stuck, and whether I was in the hallway, the cafeteria, or outside for recess, someone would find the need to call me by that nickname as they walked by. As you can imagine, this experience had a huge impact on my self-esteem. I was already self-conscious about how I looked, but the treatment from the kids at school only made things worse.

My mom did her best to encourage me by telling me not to worry about what the kids were saying about me. My stepfather attempted to help by teaching me self-defense moves in case the girls approached me again. However, their efforts weren't enough to erase the negative beliefs forming inside me about myself.

By the time I reached junior high, I walked with my head hung low and my feet dragging. I felt so ugly and wanted so much for boys to like me. Before my mom had gotten married, I had seen her go from one relationship to another, which had sent me the message that my value and worth depended on a male. I thought that if a boy liked me, it would mean I was special and worth being with. And it didn't help that I lacked words of affirmation and encouragement from a positive father-figure: my father was still in and out of jail, and I didn't see my stepfather as a father because he disrespected and mistreated my mother.

Though it might seem ironic, now that I've mentioned my step-father's teaching me self-defense, over the years, he created a tense and sometimes violent environment in the house. On the weekends, he would go out with his friends and drink, and when he came home, he would pick fights with my mother. He would explode in verbal fits of rage, waking up the household no matter what time of the night he came in. During his episodes of anger, I worried about my mother and sometimes got out of my bed to make sure she was okay. Sometimes he went through the house breaking things, causing a huge commotion. In the background I could hear my mom's calm but helpless voice pleading with him to stop. His blatant disrespect toward her irritated me and caused me to develop a deep hatred for him that would take years to heal. Clearly, there was no opportunity to develop a father-daughter bond.

So, Ms. Wholeness, as you can imagine, I felt desperate need for love and attention from a guy. As a result, I began to develop deep crushes on a few of the boys at my school. I daydreamed about being with them and wondered what it would be like to kiss them; to have them like me and want to be with me. I had not yet kissed or become intimate with a boy, unlike many of the girls in my school who had started skipping classes to have sex. I did find the nerve a few times to tell a guy that I liked him, but each time he would let me know that the feeling wasn't mutual, leaving me feeling rejected and unattractive. Not only did I admire the boys at my school, but I also admired the girls. I wanted to be like the popular girls who commanded attention and were known by all the other students. The popular girls seemed so confident and sure of themselves—characteristics I wished I possessed. The popular girls also dated the cute boys I liked, so of course I desired to be like them.

Despite the internal emotional struggle of wanting to be intimate with a boy, I still managed to make good grades in school. As time went on, I branched out and became involved with some school activities. To follow in my mom's footsteps, I joined the track team, and also became a part of the cheerleading squad. Those activities helped develop my social skills and pulled me out of my shell, which I desperately needed. While on the track team, I met and became close with one of the popular guys I had once daydreamed about. He was a great athlete and one of the best runners on the team. I was excited when he started talking to me because there was a time when he hadn't even known my name. We would laugh and joke, and I found myself really starting to like him. He even gave me his number and we would talk on the phone sometimes. He made me feel beautiful and special, like how I viewed other girls. I was so excited that he and I were talking that I thought I was going to die!

One day, after track practice, we were walking through the school and he led me to an empty stairwell, away from the rest of the team. My heart was beating rapidly with excitement because I was actually alone with him. In that stairwell I received my first kiss, and to me, it felt magical. Ms. Wholeness, I felt like I was sitting on top of the world. After that I just knew that things between him and me would progress . . . but nothing ever transpired.

Imagine my disappointment when I realized I wasn't going to become his main chick. But the kiss was enough to add a little boost to my self-esteem and give me something to brag about to my friends. Over time, I began to enjoy my junior high school years, and that feeling carried over into high school. Although the pain of my traumatic sixth-grade experience still lingered, those thoughts took a backseat as I saw myself blossom from an ugly duckling into a beautiful teenager.

By the time I reached ninth grade, I had changed my hair from the Jheri curl back to a relaxer and replaced my large-framed glasses with contact lenses. Those two enhancements made a huge difference in my appearance and boosted my self-esteem even more. Ms. Wholeness, I thought I was hot stuff because I had started getting more attention from guys at school, which is what I had always wanted. The attention increased further when I made the marching band dance team, the Vikettes, during tenth grade. I was nervous to try out because I lacked self-confidence and wasn't sure I would make it. But with the support of my mom and some of the Vikettes helping me with the routine, I made the squad. Becoming a Vikette allowed me to shake my butt in front of hundreds of students! We wore tight, short, sequined dresses; white boots with red tassels; and white gloves. We were the focal point of the band, which fit perfectly with my thirst for attention. During the pep rallies and halftime shows for the football games, I used those opportunities to really perform. Although I was surrounded by my fellow band mates, I felt like the spotlight was all on me. You see, Ms. Wholeness, my childhood lack of fatherly attention, affirmation, and love was becoming evident in my actions as a teenager. Although some of my behaviors can be attributed to just being a teen, there was also a piece of me that yearned for the male presence I was missing. Since I couldn't get fulfillment from my father or stepfather, I looked to the boys at school to fill that void.

Initially, I found myself just flirting and talking to different guys on the phone and in class, but when I found a guy I really liked, things would go a little further. We would talk on the phone more frequently, and if given the opportunity to be alone, we would become intimate, kissing and humping with clothes on. Though I enjoyed flirting with and teasing the guys, I never allowed things to go "all the way" because I took pride in the fact that I was still a virgin, while almost all my friends had started having sex.

It might seem odd, but after a couple months of talking with a guy, I would get bored and start ignoring and mistreating him. I was only able to tolerate him for a short time, and then I would be ready for someone new to come along. Ms. Wholeness, I assume that the disdain I felt for my stepfather and the lack of respect I developed for my biological father played a huge part in how I treated guys. It was easy for me to like a guy one day and be tired of him the next. I didn't trust that he would be there for me forever, so I treated him the same way I expected him to treat me. I didn't care how the guy felt because my focus was on getting the attention I was so desperate for. The experience of rejection and abandonment that resulted from my dad's inconsistent presence and my stepfather's disrespect and mistreatment of my mom had grave effects on my life and led to my difficulties overcoming these feelings. This behavior with guys carried on through the middle of my junior year.

Then I met someone who changed my life forever.

Questions for reflection:

- What pivotal moments from your childhood still impact your life today?

- How has your relationship with your parents shaped who you are today?

- How did you view yourself during your early-childhood years? How do you view yourself now?

- What is your current view of men? What male figures in your life helped shape that view?

- Do you notice an area of brokenness in light of your responses to the questions above?

Two
Could This Be Love?

During the middle of my junior year, I was introduced to a guy who would change my life in countless ways. I remember our first encounter like it was yesterday.

We had a half-day at school and would be getting out around noon. I didn't own a car, but my grandmother had let me drive hers. Because I had the freedom to go where I wanted when we got out of school, a friend from the Vikette squad and I decided to meet up with her boyfriend and another guy, whom I'll call Devin. The band had performed that morning, so we still had our tight little sequined dresses on, though we had added sweatpants and jackets for a bit more cover. When we got to my friend's boyfriend's house, the four of us sat and talked for a while. I thought Devin was kind of cute, so I was glad she had convinced me to come along. Then my friend and her boyfriend went into the back room, and Devin and I sat on the couch and talked some more. I don't remember what we said or what I was feeling. I'm sure I was shy and probably just laughed at the things he said. When my friend and her boyfriend came back to the front, she and I got ready to leave and Devin and I exchanged numbers.

Even though it seemed like we had hit it off well, a month went by before Devin and I actually talked again. I figured since he hadn't called, maybe he wasn't interested, so I didn't call him either. It didn't bother me because I had other guys to occupy my time. Then one day I saw Devin again at the mall where he worked, and we exchanged numbers again. This time he called.

We talked on the phone and got to know each other better. It didn't take long for us to get reacquainted. Shortly after the day I saw him in the mall, we devised a plan for me to come see him. My grandmother was liberal in letting me drive her car, so one day I took advantage and headed to see Devin without telling anyone. Although I had a lot of freedom at seventeen, I wasn't permitted to go visit a boy, especially when his mom wasn't home. Plus, Devin went to another school across town, so I had to cross the bridge to get to his house.

When I got there, something about him seemed different from when we had first met. There was a certain chemistry between us that I didn't remember feeling before. Since we had been talking on the phone so much, it felt like we knew each other now. I felt comfortable around him—like I could really be myself. Devin was funny and attentive, and very attractive too. We went into his room and I sat down to watch him lift weights. We talked, laughed, and joked some more, and then we ended up kissing and humping with our clothes on. It seemed so soon, but at the same time it felt right because we had developed a bond in such a short period of time.

I stayed at his house long enough to have my mom and grand-mother looking for me. Back then we didn't have cell phones, so we carried beepers, or pagers, and while I was with Devin, my mom had paged me to see where I was. I didn't want to call her from his house, so I decided to leave. I dodged the bullet of getting in trouble with my mom that day. How-ever, after that, Devin and I became inseparable. We talked for a month be-fore he asked me to be his girlfriend, and when he asked, I gladly said yes.

Ms. Wholeness, Devin was so different from the other guys I had dated because he paid attention to me and freely expressed how he felt about me. His demeanor was calm and laid back, and I felt like I could talk to him about anything. I liked the fact that I could be so free with him, and I loved that he adored me.

Devin lived with his mom and younger sister, so before we went out on our first date, my mom wanted to meet his mom and get acquainted with her. At the time, his sister was living with a relative out of town, so it felt like he was an only child like me. When our moms met, it turned out that they knew each other from high school, which created trust in terms of us visiting each other's houses. I don't remember where we went on our first date, but I was happy to be with him. It didn't take long for me to realize that Devin was my first love.

I was still a virgin when Devin and I met, but because of how I felt about him, I was considering giving him my virginity. My mom and I didn't have talks about sex. All she talked about was her desire for me to finish high school and go to college and not become a teenage mother like she did. She was adamant about me furthering my education after high school because that's something she didn't get a chance to do.

As my relationship with Devin grew, I felt it was safe to let him be my first because I loved him and desired to spend the rest of my life with him. With the absence of my dad and the disdain I carried toward my stepfather, Devin was my first experience of real love from a male, so I wanted to give him all of me. We both felt we were meant for one another and would be in each other's lives forever. It probably sounds cliché or like a story you've heard before, but at that time, in my heart and mind I couldn't see anything different.

There weren't a lot of places for teens our age to hang out at night, so most of the time, one of us would get our mom's car and we'd just ride around town so we could spend time together. We would drive to a place on the water near downtown Jacksonville and sit in the car or walk the boardwalk. We would also drive to nearby parks and empty parking lots and just sit in the car and talk. It really didn't matter to us what we did, as long as we could spend time together.

Since I had never had sex before, Devin knew penetration would be difficult, so when we were alone, he would fondle my genitals to try to loosen things up. One day, while sitting in the parking lot behind my high school, we had an intimate moment and attempted to have sex. He tried several times, but he couldn't penetrate, and the pain from the attempts was too much for me to take. We tried again on other occasions, but each time we ran into the same issue. I started to feel sad and thought that maybe something was wrong with me, especially since my friends were all having sex and didn't mention having those types of complications. In spite of our difficulties, Devin was so patient and understanding and just figured that it wasn't the right time.

Even though I loved Devin and desired to be with him, there was still a part of me that liked to get attention from other guys. It seemed like when he and I started dating, the attention from other guys increased. I still wasn't used to guys being so attentive, so I didn't have the strength or desire to resist their advances. Ms. Wholeness, I didn't realize then that they didn't have the capacity to fill the void in my life, so I continued to thirst for more attention.

I remember that one day I had my mom's car and was driving around trying to find something to do. Devin was at work, so I had time to roam the streets. One of the guys I used to talk to before dating Devin had called me earlier and asked me to come over to his house. Although I was clearly in a relationship and knew I didn't need to go over there, I figured it would be safe and that nothing would happen. So I went, and he was home alone. Now that I think about it, during that time teens spent a lot of time home alone. It's no wonder we got into so much trouble.

At first we just sat and talked. He was a real cool guy, and I was really attracted to him because he was cute, with a light brown complexion and auburn hair. I had a thing for light-skinned guys back then, and still do. He ran track, so he also had a very nice, athletic body. We started out standing outside talking, and then he invited me to come inside to see his room. Thoughts of Devin left my mind when we started kissing and humping. I was still a tease, so kissing and humping was my thing. After that, I stayed for a little while longer and then left as if nothing had ever happened.

I don't know if it was that same day or a couple of days later, but somehow, Devin found out I had gone to the guy's house. When he asked me about it, I didn't initially tell the truth because I feared losing him. However, after we talked about it more, I felt guilty and finally confessed. He was devastated. It was the first time that he and I had gotten into a disagreement about something, so I didn't know what to do. For days, he wouldn't talk to me or see me, so I had to just sit with the guilt. Knowing what I had done to Devin simply broke my heart. He was so hurt that his mom had to convince him to talk to me so we could mend things between us.

When we got back together, I vowed that I would never hurt him like that again. Although I meant it at the time, it wouldn't be the last time he heard about me being with someone else. A couple months later, I found myself repeating the same act with another guy just to get more attention. I still needed the void to be filled, and although Devin was there, he alone could not do it. Just like the first time, Devin found out about it. We went through the same process of him getting mad at me, me apologizing, and him taking me back. He always took me back, and I felt like I was indebted to him because of his forgiving heart, which made me love and respect him even more.

By this time I had transitioned into twelfth grade and was experiencing the joys of being a senior. Devin and I were still together, but we hadn't been able to reach what I felt would be the pinnacle of our relationship: sex. During this time, Devin and his mom had moved closer to where I lived, so I saw him on a more regular basis. One night, while he and I were at his house alone, we became intimate and again attempted to have sex. This time Devin was able to get all the way in. The intercourse lasted a short time, and when I got up, I saw traces of blood from my broken hymen. I ran to the bathroom and cried because I could no longer brag about being a virgin.

I had made it all the way to my senior year in high school without having sex, and in that moment, I felt all those years of saving myself were gone. I had crossed over to the other side that my friends had always talked about, and all I could think about was how sad I felt. Devin was understanding and told me it would be okay. He even apologized for being the one to take my virginity.

After a couple of days, my sadness went away and he and I began having sex more often. I didn't know it then, but our sexual relationship would eventually lead me down a destructive path.

Questions for reflection:

- Describe your experience with your first love. How did that experience shape your view of relationships?

- What decisions from your childhood have left you with guilt? What have you done with those feelings?

- If you've had sex, what memories do you have from your first experience? How has that impacted your view of sex today?

- Based on your responses, what do you notice that is still unresolved? What actions will you take to start your journey of healing in this area?

Three
Why Do I Feel So Lost?

While exploring the newness of a sexual relationship with Devin, I still managed to excel in school. Because of my scholastic achievements, I was inducted into the National Honor Society and ranked second in my high school graduating class. As a result, I was offered a full scholarship to Florida A&M University, about two hours away from my hometown.

In June of 1996, school ended and I was officially a high school graduate. The graduation was bittersweet because I had successfully completed public school but now I had to leave my many friends to begin a new adventure in college. The feeling was surreal, and the excitement and realization brought tears to my eyes.

As soon as I got home from the commencement ceremony, the excitement of my day was dampened by my stepfather and the argument he was having with my mom. He was mad at my mom because my dad had come to the graduation. For some reason, my stepfather was always jealous of my dad, which I could never understand. I guess it was the result of insecurities within himself. Whatever the reason, it added to my resentment of him.

I was supposed to go out to a graduation party and celebrate that night, but I was afraid to leave home because of his rage. I didn't want him to do something to hurt my mom. Eventually, my stepfather calmed down and it seemed the coast was clear for me to go out. A part of me still wanted to stay, but my mom convinced me to go out and have a good time. I followed her advice, went to a graduation party, and tried to enjoy myself.

I spent the rest of the summer working and preparing for my trip to college. I also made sure to spend a lot of time with Devin since we were going to be apart for so long. We were still having sex and enjoying every minute of it. I wasn't on birth control at the time and thought the "pull out" method that Devin used would keep me from getting pregnant. Plus, he had my menstrual cycle timed like clockwork, so I felt we were safe. Toward the end of the summer, I packed all of my clothes, and my family drove me to school. Devin came with us so he could send me off. It was so hard saying goodbye to him, especially since we had grown accustomed to spending so much time together. We vowed to keep in touch and make the long-distance relationship between us work.

The first year of college was an adjustment for me. It was my first time away from home for an extended period. Many of my high school classmates went to the same college as I did, but I wasn't really close to them, so I felt alone. My best friend attended Florida State University, which was right down the street, but since neither of us had cars our freshman year, we didn't get to see each other much. I talked to Devin on the phone a lot during that first year. We didn't have long-distance service on our dorm phones, so we had to use a calling card to talk to each other. We talked so much that we ran up our calling card bills, which our parents were not pleased about. I took trips home on weekends every chance I got so Devin and I could spend time together. When he could, he would come to see me and we would get a hotel room for the weekend to spend private time together.

In February, Devin made a special trip to see me for a romantic Valentine's Day weekend. That weekend would be one I would never forget, but not just for the Valentine romance. In the weeks that followed, I noticed my body starting to change, and I was eating more often than normal. When I went home for spring break, I suspected I was pregnant, so Devin took me to the store to get a pregnancy test. I remember leaving the store and stopping at a Burger King bathroom to take the test.

The test was positive.

I was in disbelief. Although we hadn't been doing anything to prevent becoming pregnant, I never thought it would happen to me.

Ms. Wholeness, I was the "good girl" who had waited until her senior year in high school to have sex. I was the first one from my immediate family to go away to college on a paid scholarship. What would happen to my scholarship? How would I be able to take care of a baby? I didn't want to leave my baby with my mom while I went to school and then come home and find that the baby didn't even recognize me as Mommy. Devin was in his last year of high school and had plans to go off to college, so how could we possibly take care of a baby? We had talked about getting married and having a family, but we weren't ready for that kind of commitment so soon.

It was an excruciating choice to make, especially since my belly had started to bulge and I was getting used to the idea of being pregnant. But it just didn't seem like the right time, so we decided I would get an abortion. When I told my mom about my pregnancy, she was upset and disappointed in me, especially since I was only nineteen and still in school. She reminded me that she hadn't wanted me to become a teenage statistic like her, so she agreed with my having an abortion. At the time, it seemed the best choice. Later, I would find out otherwise.

I remember going to the doctor for a blood test to confirm the pregnancy. They did an ultrasound and I could hear my baby's heartbeat. They gave me the printout of the sonogram and I could see a distorted view of my baby. But despite all that, we made the appointment to have the abortion. At the time, it didn't sink in with me that an actual human life was growing inside of me and needed to be protected. The only life I was trying to protect was my own.

My memory of the abortion is sketchy. I do remember feeling nervous as I sat in the waiting room with my mom and a family friend.

When they called my name, I walked back to a small room and lay down on the table. I don't recall seeing the doctor's face, but I do remember a pinching feeling as they attached a small tube to my uterus. I could hear the sound of a vacuum as they performed the suction and curettage to get my baby out. Afterward, I went into another waiting room and lounged in a recliner chair while recovering from the abortion and the medication they had given me. I felt some cramping similar to menstrual cramps.

When I finally got home, I just lay around. I felt a huge sense of emptiness and loss. I had gotten used to the swollen breasts, the constant burping, and the tiny bump in my stomach. But all of that was over now, and it was time to go back to school and continue my life as planned. What I didn't realize, Ms. Wholeness, was the impact the abortion would have on my life.

Although Devin and I stayed together after the abortion, our relationship changed. We didn't talk as much, and our trips back and forth to visit each other slacked off. My life at school changed as well, as I became more involved in extracurricular activities. I joined the Venom dance team at school and started to meet and hang out with the girls from the squad. One of them had an apartment off campus, so we would hang out there on the weekends.

While Devin and I were together long-distance, I was very loyal and didn't mess with any guys at school. One guy I had a class with was always trying to get with me. I thought he was cute, but I was in love with Devin and didn't want to mess up our relationship. However, by the end of my freshman year of college, the distance between Devin and me had taken a toll and we decided to take a break from one another. Although it was a mutual decision, I found it difficult to come to grips with the fact that he and I were no longer together. He had been my first love and the father of my aborted child, so we had a bond that was not easily severed.

Our breakup was complicated, though. When I went home for the summer, although he and I were no longer an "item," we still spent time together and continued to have sex. He had started dating someone else, so knowing that I was no longer the focus of his attention was a hard pill for me to swallow. Being with Devin had helped fill the void of not having my dad in my life, so once our relationship ended, I looked for a replacement.

When I went back to school for my sophomore year, I started to hang out with my friends and party more, which led to meeting more guys. I felt in desperate need of love, so I would do things to get attention from guys. Until sophomore year, Devin was the only guy I had slept with, but that fall, things changed quickly. By December, I had slept with five different guys, and I had found out some more devastating news . . . I was pregnant again.

Although I had slept with other guys, Devin was the only one I was having unprotected sex with, but this pregnancy turned out to be a different experience than the first one. This time, Ms. Wholeness, Devin was in another relationship, and since I was sleeping with other guys, he didn't believe the baby was his. I didn't feel the same care and concern from him as during the first pregnancy. Instead, I felt like a cheap whore, accused of not knowing who her baby's father was. In actuality, I knew Devin was the father, but that wasn't enough to convince him.

When I broke the news to my mother, she was angry. She couldn't believe I had allowed myself to go down this road again, especially now since Devin was with someone else. This pregnancy was filled with so much hurt, pain, and shame, I knew I had to end it the same way I had ended the first one. So I went to the same clinic and had another abortion.

Ms. Wholeness, I don't even remember what that abortion experience was like. It's almost as if I erased the thoughts of that one from my mind. Once again, after it was all over, I went back to school and finished out the year as if nothing had ever happened. I didn't realize that my decision had created an even deeper void that I in turn used guys to try to fill.

I deeply craved attention from guys, and they became the focal point of my life. I wanted so much to have something similar to the love Devin and I had shared. Even though he had moved on, a part of me still held on to the hope that he and I would one day get back together. But near the end of my sophomore year, I received news that shattered those hopes and broke my heart into a million pieces: Devin's sister called and told me that the girl he was with had gotten pregnant and they had decided to get married.

This news left me broken—not only because my first love was getting married to someone else, but also because he was having a baby while I was left with the guilt and shame of the two babies I had aborted. It seemed so unfair that he got the opportunity to have a child while I was left with the possibility of not being able to conceive again. I felt my heart had been ripped out of my chest and I didn't know how to restore it.

I internalized the hurt and acted out by becoming very promiscuous. I reached a point of not caring anymore, not respecting my body or seeing any value or worth in myself.

Remember the guy I mentioned earlier who was trying to get with me my freshman year? Well, after realizing that things were definitely over between Devin and me, I decided to give him a chance. We slept together and I fell hard for him. We would talk on the phone, and he would come by and visit. He even wrote me a letter during the summer after our sophomore year, which I thought was so sweet! I was glad to hear from him. However, he wrote that he wasn't ready to be in a relationship. He said he thought I was definitely "the girlfriend type" and that he would be with me once he was ready to settle down. I held on to that and waited on him. I really liked him because he was cute, with a nice body, as well as a bit of a thuggish side.

But when we got back to school for junior year, I didn't hear from him much. I would call repeatedly, only to get his voicemail, and he did not often return my calls. Later I found out he had met a freshman and they had become a couple. Again, I was devastated: for the second time a guy had chosen another woman over me. This further deepened my feelings of worthlessness and of not being good enough to be someone's "main girl."

By this time I had moved off campus to a townhouse with two of my close friends, which allowed me the freedom to really do what I wanted. I had stopped dancing with the dance team and decided to join one of the modeling troupes on campus. I participated in fashion shows, which was a perfect way to get more attention. I modeled the latest casual, business, and couture fashions, but I especially liked the lingerie scenes where I could flaunt my body in skimpy clothes and have guys lust over me. Ms. Wholeness, I was so lost, spiraling down a destructive path that would lead to nothing but a dead end.

While in the modeling group, I met a guy named Ronnie, and we began to talk and have sex. Ronnie was cute, fine, and popular, so I developed strong feelings for him very quickly. I wanted to be in an exclusive relationship with him, but just like my previous romantic interest, he said he wasn't ready for a commitment. He too talked about what a good person he thought I was and how when he was ready to settle down, he would choose me. Sounds familiar, right?

I spent weekends at his house and we had a lot of fun. We flirted during modeling rehearsals and even went on a few dates. The way things were going, I thought for sure that it wouldn't be long before he and I were a couple. I even remember being with him a few times and wanting him to get me pregnant so I could have a baby. After my second abortion, I felt so empty and vowed that I would never terminate a pregnancy again. I wanted to have a baby intentionally to "make up for" aborting my two children. But my plan with Ronnie didn't work out.

After a few months, things between us fell apart and our relationship ended. I found out he had started dating one of the other girls in our modeling troupe, Keisha, and things between them were getting pretty serious. Again, I was deeply hurt because this would make the third time that a guy had chosen someone else over me. Once again I internalized it and took it to mean that I wasn't good enough.

As you can imagine, Ms. Wholeness, my sense of self-esteem had been flushed down the toilet. I felt unworthy of being number one in a guy's life. I felt like all I was good for was being someone's "chick on the side" while everything within me desired to be the first priority. I felt rejected and abandoned by my dad because of his absence while I was growing up, and the same feelings surfaced after Devin, the guy from my class, and now Ronnie.

Since Keisha was a part of our modeling "family," I had to see her and Ronnie together, which ate me up inside. On top of that, Keisha was really sweet and she and I became good friends. She knew Ronnie and I used to mess around before she came along, but I reassured her that things between us were over and I was cool with them being together. The real truth was that I still had feelings for him that would not easily go away. So even though they were together, he and I would still flirt when no one else was around. A part of me felt bad because Keisha was really nice and trusted me as a friend, but I was so torn and broken on the inside that I allowed my selfishness to take control. I still messed with other guys, but deep down inside I wanted to be with Ronnie.

One day, after we had been flirting with each other in rehearsal, Ronnie came over to my house and ended up staying until the early hours of the morning. During this time, he and Keisha were living together, and I later found out she had spent all night riding around looking for him. The next day she confided in me and told me what had happened. I felt so low-down and dirty because I knew where he had been but couldn't find it in my heart to tell her. At that moment, I had reached the lowest low, allowing my deep longing for love to betray a good friend. I felt horrible and dirty. It was like I was on a merry-go-round of destruction and couldn't get off. I thought I was the worst person in the world and that I could never change.

One day I was sitting in the living room of our townhouse, thinking about what I had done to Keisha, and the pain I felt brought me down to my knees in prayer. I cried out to God for help. I needed Him to change the monster I had become. I knew that my actions didn't reflect who I really was, but I didn't know how to change.

I had been attending church off and on, but after betraying Keisha, I decided to start going more regularly. When I went, it felt like the preacher was speaking directly to me. After going a few times, I went up to the front of the church during the altar call and rededicated my life to God. I had grown up in church and accepted Jesus Christ as my Lord and Savior when I was younger, but I didn't have a relationship with God. Recommitting my life was the first step in establishing a true relationship with Him. I needed change in my life because by this time, I had slept with over thirty guys and had contracted STDs. If I kept traveling down the path I was on, I was going to die without ever fulfilling my life's purpose.

After that last incident with Ronnie, I stopped messing with him and felt like my life was slowly taking a change for the better. I started going to Bible Study at church and even signed up to join the choir. Now, Ms. Wholeness, I will be honest and say that all of my promiscuous behavior didn't stop once I rededicated my life to God. Although God can do the miraculous, my change didn't happen overnight. It was a gradual process that wasn't easy. At times I still gave in to tempting situations, but somehow things seemed different. I started to feel convicted and no longer enjoyed myself.

By this time I had entered my senior year of college and had started to go on job interviews. I was experiencing mixed emotions about the interviews and finding a job because a part of me felt invincible, like I could do anything, while another part of me felt discouraged, worthless, and incapable of succeeding. The latter feelings seemed like a strong force holding me back from being all that I could be. I was doing just enough to get by in school while not setting my goals high enough to achieve excellence. I couldn't decipher whether I was experiencing laziness or fear. Whatever it was, I knew I had to fight through it.

The spring of my senior year, I had interviewed with a federal agency in Arlington, Virginia. When my mom called to say they had sent a letter to my home address offering me the position, I was super-excited because they were the last company I had interviewed with and I was starting to lose hope about finding a job. I was also excited because I always wanted to live up north where it snowed, so I felt like God had blessed me with this opportunity. This was my chance to start a new life and leave my past behind.

In April of 2001, I graduated with a bachelor's degree in accounting, and after spending a month in my hometown of Jacksonville, I packed my things and moved to Virginia.

Questions for reflection:

- What relationship breakups have you experienced that took you a long time to recover from? Are there any unresolved emotions?

- What low moment in life caused you to reach the end of yourself and desire to change?

- If you've accepted Jesus as your Savior, what prompted you to make that decision? If you haven't, but desire to, turn to the Afterword of this book.

- Based on your responses, what do you notice that is still unresolved? What actions will you take to start your journey of healing in this area?

Four
Can God Really Change Me?

My mom knew about my abortions, but she had no idea about my promiscuous lifestyle and how dark things had gotten in my life. Honestly, Ms. Wholeness, I was too ashamed to tell her because it would probably have broken her heart. So as we drove from Florida to Virginia, I kept those secrets to myself.

During our apartment search in Virginia, my mom and I stumbled across a large apartment complex in Alexandria, about six miles from where I would be working. It looked like a safe environment, so we found a vacant one-bedroom I could move into and call home. I was excited about living by myself since I had spent my college years with roommates. In a new community, where nobody knew who I was or where I had come from, it seemed like the perfect opportunity to start afresh and begin a new chapter of my life.

Well, Ms. Wholeness, I didn't realize how much not having room-mates would leave me alone with my thoughts. I wasn't prepared to be haunted by everything I had done up until that point. Yes, I had left my college life behind, but I couldn't run away from the real problem, which was *me*. So my first year living in Alexandria was rough.

As I sat in solitude much of the time those first few weeks, I thought about myself and wondered what kind of person I really was. I recalled all the things I had done to hurt people, especially men, and how I would meet them and then throw them away when I found something that I didn't like about them. In some cases, I would com-pletely stop talking to them without thinking twice about it. I also thought about how I had betrayed Keisha by continuing to sleep with Ronnie while they were together. I hated who I was and wished I could be someone else. I wanted to be someone who had it all together and was content and at peace with herself. I concluded that the way I had treated some of the men I messed with was the result of how my dad and other guys in my life had treated me. They couldn't see the value in me, so they made promises they couldn't keep, or they used me and then discarded me like I was nothing.

Ms. Wholeness, there was so much going on in me at that time. I still had a deep desire to be loved by a guy, so I couldn't go anywhere without wondering if that would be the day or the place I would meet my next boyfriend. I was uncovering so many issues within myself that needed to be worked on that I didn't know where to begin. I knew that I needed to turn to God, but I had reached a place in my spiritual relationship where

I couldn't pray or read my Bible. A strong force was holding me back from reaching out to God for help. The force was telling me to keep trying to handle my issues on my own. I now realize it was the devil trying to keep me isolated and bound.

I spent a lot of my days back then feeling depressed and crying for no apparent reason. During my sad moments, all I wanted to do was sit and listen to slow R&B music and cry until my problems went away. Crying made me feel better. Little did I know that God was aware of my sorrows and collecting every tear (Psalm 56:8).

After starting my new job, I made a few friends at work who were really nice and welcoming. One of them invited me to attend her church, which happened to be right down the street from where I lived. On the first day I visited the church, I ended up joining and becoming a member. I hadn't planned to join, but the choir started singing a song that I happened to be listening to on the way to the church, so I figured it was a sign from God that this was where I needed to be. The church was small and family-oriented, so they made me feel welcome. It was the type of family atmosphere that I needed, since my family was ten hours away. After joining the church, I started to attend Bible Study and other activities and events the church hosted, which helped me to get out of the house and focus on something other than myself.

I was struggling with the fact that by this point I'd had premarital sex with thirty-five different guys, with confusion about who I was, and with my lack of faith and trust in God. Although I had rededicated my life to God before leaving college, at times I still felt disconnected from Him and knew that I wasn't being obedient to the way He desired for me to live. I wanted desperately to separate myself from the lifestyle I had been living, but I found it so difficult to let go of old habits. I prayed that God would strengthen me so I could grow and have a closer relationship with Him. I wanted God to do something new in my life, and it turned out He did just that.

As New Year 2003 approached, I had been working in Arlington for a year and a half, and I decided to pursue a graduate degree to stimulate my mind and keep me from being lazy. The church I was attending also wanted to kick off the new year with a fresh start, so they designated January as a month of consecration during which members of the church were to fast from eating from six a.m. to six p.m. Now, Ms. Wholeness, I had never gone on a fast before, so I thought to myself, "There is no way I can handle that." Back then I only weighed 100 pounds, so I couldn't imagine not eating for twelve hours a day for a whole month! But after thinking and praying about it for a couple weeks, I decided to give it a try. I started fasting around mid-month, and the experience was the best I had ever had. I read scriptures and prayed throughout the day and intentionally focused on God, which created a deeper connection to Him.

During the first week of my fast, my secret about Ronnie and me messing around while he was with Keisha finally came out. Keisha randomly called me one day to ask if I knew anything about Ronnie that I hadn't told her. She and Ronnie were still together, but she felt that something wasn't right about their relationship and had decided to call me and ask since we all used to be in the same group. I knew it was no coincidence that this was coming out during this fast, and I trusted that God was helping me to cleanse my heart of the things from my past that were weighing me down. So I admitted to her what had happened and apologized for betraying her. After we got off the phone, I knew the news had stung her heart, and that made me sad. But I was thankful that I could finally release that secret and the devil could no longer use it to torment me.

Also during the fast, I had a sexual encounter with a guy who lived in Alexandria but whom I had met online. He had been out of town for a couple weeks and happened to come back while I was on the fast. When I went to see him, I ended up falling into temptation and having sex with him. But, Ms. Wholeness, the weirdest thing happened while we were in the middle of the act. My body didn't react to him the way it normally did during sex, and he and I both could tell that something was wrong. He was also a Christian and stated that maybe God was trying to tell us something. I agreed and suggested we stop and pray about the situation and repent of the sin we had just committed. After that encounter, we went our separate ways, which was something I needed to do anyway.

Although I only participated in the fast for half the month, during that short time God answered so many of my prayers. I could truly begin to see the gradual changes in my life and the growth in my relationship with God.

Ms. Wholeness, God was truly bringing about a change in me, but one of the things I have learned on my journey with God is that when you start making progress and breaking away from old habits and thought patterns, a struggle takes place that makes moving forward more difficult. Right at the time when I was ready to take a break from men and focus on my relationship with God, I met a guy named Tony. It was the last week of the fast, while I was attending a meeting for a young professionals network-ing group. Tony was charming, attentive, and funny. He was a Christian too, so he invited me to attend Bible Study with him. I was amazed because it was the first time I had met a guy who attended church and seemed to have a relationship with God. I knew I needed to be alone with God and didn't need to be in a romantic relationship, but I reasoned that maybe Tony was a blessing to my life and we would be able to help each other grow in Christ.

Tony had recently gotten out of a long-term relationship, so he wasn't interested in pursuing another one right away. But that didn't stop us from spending time together. We felt that we would just start as friends and go with the flow. But that friendship boundary was violated a couple of weeks later when we became sexually intimate. At that point I knew that things between us would change. I was disappointed in myself because just when I had made the decision to give relationships a break and spend some alone time with God, I allowed myself to get entangled in another relationship. I felt I couldn't help myself. At the time, I didn't have the strength to resist attention and affection from a man.

After Tony and I crossed that line, things between us progressed quickly, and in a short time, we became a couple. Despite our choice to sin, I liked the feeling of having a boyfriend, especially since I had not been in a committed relationship since Devin. Tony was so expressive of his feelings, which I wasn't used to. He told me how he felt about me, wrote me poems, and even mentioned the idea of us spending the rest of our lives together if that was God's plan. Things between us appeared to be going well. However, deep inside I was unhappy because I knew what I was doing did not please God.

God was doing such great things in my life; He had blessed me with the desire to go back to school, and had placed in my heart a calling to start a dance ministry at my church. Though I had always danced at school, this would be the first time I had devoted that talent to God. I didn't know much about liturgical dance or leading a ministry, but I was willing to give it a try because it was heavy on my heart. It was also something Tony had encouraged me to do.

So while all of those good things were going on in my life, in my heart I felt like I was messing up again by continuing to have sex and not totally focusing my life on God. I wanted to do what was right, but I found it so easy to go back to what was wrong. I prayed that God would help me and show me how to turn years of doing wrong into doing right. Ms. Wholeness, that was the prayer I prayed, and though I didn't realize it at the time, God was already answering it.

While in the relationship with Tony, I learned some things about myself. I learned that I was struggling with abandonment issues, which came out one night when Tony was over. He had spent the entire day with me, but when it was time for him to go, I started to cry. He wasn't leaving to go out of town or leaving to walk out of my life; he was just leaving to go home. It was the first time I had cried about something like this, but it let me know that I had some deep unresolved issues.

I also realized how desperately I wanted to have a baby. Tony and I weren't using contraceptives—just the "pull out" method. A couple of times I suggested that he and I try to make a baby, but he didn't like that idea. I guess it was a blessing that we didn't because I started to notice things about Tony that I didn't like. I realized that he promised to do a lot, but rarely followed through. He wasn't reliable, dependable, or a good communicator, and those qualities were important to me. I also saw that his relationship with God wasn't as genuine as I had thought, and through the course of our conversations, I noticed that the things we desired spiritually were starting to differ. We weren't of one accord anymore: I still desired to get closer to God, while he was more focused on doing his own thing. I still hoped that God could use me as a witness for Him.

I made myself believe that Tony was the one for me, and I determined to make our relationship work. He was falling, and I believed it was my responsibility to lift him up. But a few days after I started having those thoughts, Tony decided we needed to take a break. He had recently lost his job and felt he needed some time by himself. The news wasn't a shock because he had already stopped coming over like he normally would. I used his absence to focus more on my relationship with God. It seemed that God was preparing me for our breakup.

When our relationship did actually end, I thought I would be crying all over the place and grieving, but I wasn't, so I questioned whether I had really loved Tony. I wondered if I had really had strong feelings for him or if he was just another guy I had used to fill a void in my life. Those questions intensified when, not long after our breakup, I noticed a guy who attended my friend's church and wanted to know more about him. It seemed weird that I could just move on so quickly, especially since, deep down inside, I felt that I needed some healing. At that time, I didn't know what I needed healing *from*, but I did recognize that I had some issues.

I tried to think of slick ways to get the guy's attention. He was a Christian and totally committed to God. My friend told me some great things about him, which made me even more interested. I thought about sending him an email to say hello, but I decided that would be too forward. I noticed my new attraction to young Christian men, especially because they were rare in my age group—mid-twenties. I remember also having a crush on the young pastor of a local church who was the same age as me. I mentally devised a few plans to get him to notice me, but I caught myself and dismissed the thoughts. I prayed that God would help me get it together.

Although I was still having issues letting go of men, I felt myself thinking more about God. I woke up with Him on my mind and desired to spend more time with Him. One night I remember having a dream that one of my friends was trying to kill me. As she pointed a gun at me, I stood there boldly and was not afraid. She shot the gun three times, but none of the bullets hit me. From the dream I gathered that nothing would be able to harm me when I put my trust in God. But once again, Ms. Wholeness, as my relationship with God started to grow, other thoughts competed for my attention.

I started to think about Tony and wondered if he had found someone else. I thought back to the moment while Tony and I were still together when I believed that God had told me Tony would be my husband. I had been walking from my job to the subway station to catch the train home, and thinking about nothing other than how cold it was. Then, all of a sudden, the words "Tony will be your husband" popped into my mind. I figured it had to be God speaking. So although Tony was saying he needed space, I was sure things between us would work out somehow.

Now a few months had passed since our breakup, and I had moved from Virginia to Maryland and was living with two friends from work. We all had a desire to grow spiritually and live pure and holy lives. Tony had found a job and moved to Maryland by then too, so I thought for sure that we would get back together. But my hopes were shattered when I recalled how he talked a good game but didn't back it up with actions. I decided it really was time for me to move on, and I thanked God for not allowing us to get back together. Looking back now, I know that letting go of Tony was truly a blessing.

By the time 2004 rolled around, I felt it was a chance to start over. I prayed that God would help me live a life of abstinence. I wanted to get to the point where I didn't allow another man to violate my body. I wanted to save myself for marriage so I could have something to give to my future husband. But about two weeks after I prayed that prayer, I ended up having sex with a guy I worked with. My spirit was willing to do the right thing, but I hadn't learned self-control and how to resist temptation.

To make matters worse, the guy had a girlfriend, so I knew that the only thing I could be to him was a side chick. Once again I had allowed myself to be second in someone's life. Imagine the strange dichotomy of seeing yourself changing but still being haunted by a part of your past. It left a residue of discouragement and doubt that I could never escape. Like a little child watching her friends play while she was stuck inside, I saw other people growing spiritually and getting in relationships that led to marriage, while I felt stagnant. The remedy I heard others use was to read the Bible and pray more, but at the time I didn't have the faith to trust God enough to give the situations I was struggling with over to Him completely.

In the midst of this internal struggle, I was leading the dance ministry at church and felt more of a desire to dance. One day I woke up at four a.m. with choreography to the song "The Anointing," by John P. Kee, going through my mind. In my head, a woman's melodious voice sang with such power and conviction that I felt commanded to illustrate each move visually. God was going to use this creative gift of ministry to free a lot of people from their struggles, starting with me!

Times like these were when I felt really connected to God and saw Him working in and through me. Ms. Wholeness, it may seem weird that while I was struggling with sin, God was still using me to minister to others, but that's just how He works. I know it wasn't a good idea that I was continuing to have sex while leading a ministry, but it just goes to show that God can use us even in our mess. We are imperfect beings, so waiting to serve Him until we have it all together is pointless. I believe God can use us mightily when we humble ourselves and seek Him for help in the midst of our flaws.

I wanted to read the Bible more because I had heard people talk about the importance of that practice for everyday living. I had been praying about it, and one day God answered my prayers. I was sitting in church and heard a small voice within that said, "Teach." I thought to myself, "What? Teach? I don't even read the Bible, so how am I supposed to teach it?" But then I thought, "Hmmm . . . In order to teach, I will have to study so I can effectively present what the scriptures say. Maybe that's how God is answering my prayers about reading more!"

Out of curiosity, I obeyed the voice, went to the superintendent of the Sunday school program at our church, and told her I felt God calling me to teach. She was excited because they needed teachers for the teen Sunday school class. She gave me the materials to prepare and told me I could start in a few months. I ran home and jumped right into the materials like a kid in a candy store. Reading the lessons and learning about different people in the Bible brought me so much joy! I couldn't wait to share what I was learning with the students in my class.

I began to see that everything I needed was in the Bible and that reading it provided me with new revelation and understanding about God.

I guess God knew I would have this reaction to His command to teach. I'm glad I listened and obeyed.

My relationship with God was blossoming, but that didn't curb the deep desire I still had to be with a man. And then I met William . . .

Questions for reflection:

- Has there been a moment that caused a turning point in your life? If so, what was it?

- How do you feel about yourself today? What contributed to that view of yourself?

- Have you ever reached a point where you couldn't pray or read your Bible? What caused you to get there?

- Is there an area of your life that you feel you need to clean up before God can use you? What makes you feel that way?

- Based on your responses, what do you notice that is still unresolved? What actions will you take to start your journey of healing in this area?

Five
What Do I Do with My Baggage?

William and I were introduced in July of 2004 through one of my fellow church members. She approached me one day after church and said, "I have a co-worker who is a very nice guy that I think would be perfect for you. Do you mind if I give him your number?" At the time I was still hung up on a guy I had been communicating with who was in jail, but I liked the idea of meeting new people, so I said, "Sure." Shortly after that, he and I talked for a short time and the conversation piqued my interest. Since we hadn't yet met in person, we agreed to go out on a date. I was nervous at first and didn't know what to expect, but I remembered my church member's description of him as handsome, nice, and poised, so that put me at ease.

When William arrived at my house for our date, it was pouring rain. One of my roommates was looking out the window trying to get a peek at him before he got to the door. At first he didn't get out of the car, so she said, "I know he doesn't expect you to go out there in the rain." I was thinking the same thing. But he eventually got out, grabbed an umbrella, and came to the door.

My first impression was that he was okay-looking. He was dark-skinned, tall, and slim, which was different than the guys with lighter complexions that I was more attracted to. But I figured I wouldn't let my preferences hinder me from getting to know him. He was nicely dressed and appeared to be a gentleman because he walked me to the car under his umbrella so I wouldn't get wet. I found out later that as a precautionary measure, my roommate had written down his description and license plate number just in case he wasn't the gentleman he seemed to be. I appreciated her concern and support. Ms. Wholeness, it's so important that, as women, we look out for each other.

On the way to dinner, I noticed that William's demeanor was different from that of the guys I normally dated. I was used to the more "hood" or "tough" type guys, but William appeared to be a different breed. He was more polished and gentle, which concerned me initially and caused me to question his intentions. However, on our date we conversed a lot and I saw how much we had in common. I confessed that I was a Christian and wanted to develop a friendship first and allow it to blossom into a relationship, which I admitted was something I hadn't learned to do. I explained how fast my past relationships had progressed to being intimate and that I wanted to try a new approach, without intimacy. He admitted that he had never been in a relationship without the intimacy but was willing to give it a try. He, too, believed that developing a friendship was important, so he agreed with that approach.

Ms. Wholeness, intellectually I knew I wanted to develop friendship first. It was something my mom would always say when I told her I had met someone new. It sounded like something I wanted to try out. But underneath my intellect was so much emotional baggage that hadn't been unpacked, in addition to no clear model of what developing a friendship with a guy looked like. Without that model, and with all of my emotional baggage still on board, my mind defaulted to old ways of thinking. So after great conversation and sharing similar interests on that first date, my mind fast-forwarded to the future and what might happen between us. I despised the fact that I was so hasty in wanting to pursue something deeper, especially after only knowing the guy for a short time. But my voids were thirsting for the next man to fill me up, so any sign of attraction caused me to rush things along in my mind and fantasize about us being together. It was almost like I was a "junkie" for attention from men, so when they gave me the "fix" of good conversation, laughter, and quality time, I felt an emotional high and immediately wanted more. It created an intoxicating feeling that I couldn't get enough of. So, it was no surprise that I had that sort of intoxicating experience on the first date with William.

One thing I noticed that was different about William was that he didn't shower me with compliments about how good I looked, like other guys normally did when we first met. That seemed odd and created a mystery about him that I wanted to know more about.

It had been a couple of weeks since William and I had gone out on our first date. We had talked over the phone, but he never mentioned seeing me again. Again, that was odd and different from other guys, but instead of sitting back and waiting for him to say something, I figured I needed to initiate the next meeting. During one of our conversations, I suggested that William let me come over and cook dinner for him. I was used to doing things to please men, so I figured if I cooked for William, he would see what a great woman I was and would want to claim me as his own. Once again, I had bypassed friendship and was scheming to get in a relationship.

When I got to his house I was amazed at how nice it was! He owned his home, and it was clean, nicely decorated, and fully furnished. I fell in love with it and immediately felt at home there when he first showed me around. It was nice to see a black man handling his business. He was successful, educated, and not bad looking, so on paper he seemed like the perfect candidate for me. I cooked a good meal for him and we had a nice time conversing and getting to know each other more, but I thought it was still weird that he hadn't complimented me or said anything about how he felt about me. I needed that verbal admission of attraction so I could feel wanted and desired by a man and use my body to hook him in even more. But I dismissed the thoughts and figured he would express himself one day. Ms. Wholeness, I really wanted to get out of the mode of thinking about relationships so I could allow things to flow into a friendship, but it was difficult, especially when I was in the company of someone I was interested in. I figured I just needed to be patient, keep reading the Bible, and pray.

The weekend after our second date, I went home to Florida to visit my family. My visits home always seemed like a test of my faith and a measuring stick for how much I had grown. During this particular weekend, I visited a guy I had known for years. I got weak and we ended up having sex. Ms. Wholeness, I was so disappointed in myself because I had been doing really well with abstaining. The next day I hung out with another guy I had gone to school with, and even though we didn't have sex, we had an intimate moment with each other. Abstaining from sex after being active for years felt like trying to tame a wild beast. I was like a caged bird that desperately wanted to be free. Those two individuals fed the "beast" and gave me the "fix" of attention, flattering words, and physical touch that I was lacking with William. I rationalized that William was the answer to my prayers to know friendship with a man and that God was teaching me patience and how to move at a slower pace with the opposite sex. However, this perceived "patience test" was killing me!

It had been about a month since William and I first went out, and nothing had transpired like I was used to. Unlike the other guys, he was the type of man that I couldn't have my way with. I wanted to see him more often, but I wanted him to be the one to pursue me. There was an impatient and controlling nature within me that wanted to take the lead and get what I wanted. But at the same time, this was the perfect situation for me to calm down and learn to take things slow. Then I thought to myself, "It's only been a month, so why am I tripping already?"

It was exciting to be experiencing something new, but frustrating because it seemed foreign. It was the first time I was attracted to a guy without my emotions being all caught up into him or distorted by sex. So to keep from messing up the flow of our friendship, I resisted the moments when I wanted to mention seeing him again. I suppressed how I felt so I could allow him to take the lead. He was five years older than me, so I figured he could teach me a thing or two about relationships. Up until this point, my connections with men had been shallow—not rooted in anything deep or lasting. I hadn't learned how to develop aspects of a relationship such as communication and trust. William challenged me to talk about other things that do not relate to sex.

I could see the benefit of being with William, but I couldn't deny that I wanted things to go a little faster. I found myself on what felt like an emotional pendulum, swinging back and forth between patience and frustration. About a month and a half into our friendship, I was getting frustrated with both William and myself, and was about to call it quits. The main reason was that I didn't feel I could be the loyal friend that he needed me to be. Basically, Ms. Wholeness, I didn't feel like I was good enough for William. I considered myself too jacked up to do right by him. Those feelings magnified after I got together with Tony. He had called out of the blue one day and suggested we go out to dinner. I honestly didn't believe he was serious because he'd said that before, but he actually followed through this time.

During dinner we got caught up on how things were going in our lives and even flirted with each other a little, but that was about it. We didn't talk about getting back together or being intimate after dinner. I no longer had feelings for Tony, but just seeing how I could dismiss my feelings for William and hang out with my ex made me feel that I didn't know how to be a true friend. However, that thought didn't last long because a couple days after my dinner with Tony, William *finally* asked me out on another date! I could tell he was becoming more comfortable and trusting with me, so I didn't want to hurt him or take his slow-paced process for granted. From that point on, I made sure that William was the only guy I was seeing so I could prove to myself that I was a faithful and loyal friend.

Ms. Wholeness, I had such good intentions, but I allowed my emotions to be the driver for my decisions, and that created so much drama in my life. By the time William and I reached the two-month mark in our friendship, I was back on the frustrated side of my internal pendulum and decided to break things off. I reasoned that I didn't have to settle when I knew deep down in my heart that I wanted something else. I felt like I shouldn't be afraid to let go of trying to be in control, and just needed to wait on God to send me what I truly desired.

About a week after I ended things with William, I was convinced that I was starting a period of long-suffering and starting to go through a process a lot like withdrawal. I suffered from loneliness and questioned if I would ever find true love. I wondered, "Now that I'm by myself, what on earth am I supposed to think about that doesn't involve a man? Men have consumed my thinking for as long as I can remember, so what am I supposed to do with my life now? God, how can you transform a mind like mine that is so resistant to change?" I just wanted to sit in my room and cry because I couldn't get my way or dodge the process that God was taking me through. I wanted to cry because I knew I had to endure and I didn't know what else to do. . . .

Oh, Ms. Wholeness, I'll be the first to admit that the mind renewal process is not easy to go through. It's difficult because during that time, God is pruning and refining us and removing those thoughts, attitudes, and behaviors that aren't like Him. It's a process that continues until the day we leave this earth. The Bible says in Romans 12:2, "Don't copy the behavior and customs of this world, but let God transform you into a new person by changing the way you think. Then you will know what God wants you to do, and you will know how good and pleasing and perfect his will really is." When we accept Jesus as our

Savior and secure our salvation with God, He works within us to remove the old habits and sinful ways that we had before giving our lives to Christ, so our lives can resemble the life of Jesus. The more we yield ourselves and our will during this transformation process, the more God can do in and through us. But when we don't give ourselves to be transformed, we hinder what God can do in our lives. So even though the mind renewal process is difficult, it's necessary in order to grow spiritually and to mature as a person. I wanted to get closer to God, and I knew the only way to Him was to allow myself to go through the mind renewal process. But just like a drug addict being weaned from their addiction, it's a process that requires taking things day by day. Men were my drug, so it would require me to go through the process to get weaned from my addiction.

Two days after I decided to surrender myself to God's renewing of my mind, William and I went out on another date. He had already bought the tickets to the event before I decided to end things between us, so I would have felt bad for not going. I didn't realize that this would make it more difficult for me to stick to my plan of being by myself. To make matters worse, since we had last seen one another, he had upgraded his vehicle and purchased a luxury car. I wasn't the type to be driven by material things, but the fact that he had added the car to his résumé made it difficult for me to ignore that this brother had it going on. As a result of our date, I felt even more lonely, confused, and unsure of what I wanted. One minute I was thinking I shouldn't be with him, and the next minute I felt that I should. I wanted to say things to express how I felt about him, but I didn't know if my feelings were genuine or coming from a place of neediness and loneliness. So I held back my feelings because I just wasn't sure.

The day after our date, I concluded that my emotional distress was just the devil trying to keep me away from what I truly deserved. I blamed the devil for trying to convince me to think things about William that weren't true. I felt that God had placed William in my life to show me what a real man looked like. Actually, Ms. Wholeness, all I was doing was justifying my way back to a place of comfort. I rationalized why it was okay for me to reconnect with William and felt that God was leading me to do so. But the truth is, I was being led by my emotions and just wasn't ready to be by myself. Oftentimes we blame things that we just don't want to face or do on the devil. So I allowed myself to keep swinging on the emotional pendulum and get back with William, not knowing where I would end up next.

About two weeks after I decided to reconnect with William and three months after we first met, I was also starting to reconnect with my feelings of loneliness. At that time, William was out of town and I really missed him. I didn't understand why, because he wasn't very affectionate and we didn't spend much time together. Nevertheless, I desired a passionate kiss or a warm hug and to have him look in my eyes and tell me the sweet and sentimental things I needed to hear. I was like an emotional balloon that was ready to explode because I had so many feelings bottled up inside that I couldn't release. There was so much passion and love inside of me just waiting for the opportunity for me to shower them on that special someone. Once again, I suppressed my feelings because I thought they were the result of my deeply rooted issues. No one told me that there was some validity to the way I was feeling and that many of the things I wanted were natural desires. I just figured something was desperately wrong with me and that my neediness and internal issues were solely to blame. I was being tortured by my own thoughts and beliefs.

Even though I knew after three months that William and I weren't compatible, I stayed with him for five years, hoping, praying, and wishing for things to change. I needed something to keep me hanging on. I rationalized what I was feeling and wanted to be open with him, but I was so afraid that he would see me for who I was and not like the real me. One night we had a heart-to-heart talk and I learned that he was just looking for a woman he could trust and let his guard down with. At the core, he was a good man. He respected me and throughout the five years, never tried to have sex with me. When I asked him why, he said, "You said you were used to being intimate in your past relationships and wanted something different. I was trying to show you something different." Indeed, no matter how many times I tried to go against my own word and tempt him, he never gave in, which I truly appreciated. At times it seemed like we were getting closer; at other times it seemed like we were so distant, even though we only lived a few miles apart. He would always tell me it was important to be friends first to create the foundation for a strong relationship. But after five years I thought, "How much more *friends* do we need to be?"

I was longing for William to give me the love I truly desired, but deep down inside I knew that God was the only one who could fill the voids in my soul. All the words, actions, and thoughts of a man couldn't fill the emptiness within me. I tried to deny, avoid, and ignore the small whispers within that kept saying, "Deal with *you*." I knew that I needed to, but I just didn't know how. What was I supposed to do to "deal with me"? Pray? Read? Do something differently? I was sick and tired of being sick and tired! I wanted to love who I was and be content with where I was in life. God had truly blessed me, but because of the mindset I was in, I couldn't enjoy those blessings.

At the time I didn't believe I could be open and honest about these things with the women around me, so I kept a lot of my feelings to myself and just wrote in my journal. Little did I know that years later God would call me to share my experiences with you, Ms. Wholeness, in hopes that my story of healing would also help you to heal. Back then I thought that if anyone knew what was really going on in my head, they would think I had lost my mind. The emotional ups and downs, indecisiveness, insecurities, and confusion had me in a constant whirlwind.

After five years of pursuing William and trying to get him to love me the way I desired, I got tired and gave up. I didn't have anything left to give. I couldn't believe that I was going back to the drawing board and starting over after all of the energy, time, and emotions I had invested in that relationship. But I had reached my breaking point and it was time to let go. Instead of calling him on the phone to explain for the hundredth time that I felt we needed to break up, I took the easy way out and sent him a text message saying we needed to go our separate ways. I was solely focused on my own emotions, so I wasn't concerned about how he felt or what he thought. I was done. Looking back on it now, I know that wasn't the best approach, but that's just where I was at the time.

After ending such a long-term relationship, I knew, once again, I needed time to heal, and part of me wanted time to myself. It made sense logically to take a break before trying to move forward, but my heart also felt deprived of love, attention, and affection. So it's not surprising that I began to converse more with my friend Jeff within the same week I broke up with William. I needed another "attention dealer" so I could get another "fix."

Questions for reflection:

- Have you ever felt like you were not good enough to be with someone? Why?

- When have you allowed your emotions to take the lead in your relationship decisions? What was the outcome?

- What are your relationship patterns? Is there anything about these patterns that needs to be changed?

- Based on your responses, what do you notice that is still unresolved? What actions will you take to start your journey of healing in this area?

Six

What Do I Do When All Hell Breaks Loose?

Jeff and I met in college during my sophomore year, on the social media site College Club, which was popular back then. His profile picture was of him at the beach with his shirt off, rubbing one eye. I was immediately drawn to his light complexion, his thick muscular build, and the cool tattoo on his chest. We had a class together and I had always thought he was attractive, but I had never said anything. So seeing him on the site was my opportunity to spark a conversation. We started chatting online and later decided to meet in person. He was really nice, and different from the other guys I had been talking to because he was attentive and didn't appear to just want me for sex. He actually wanted to talk and spend quality time together. He called me a lot, which was different for me because I had grown accustomed to being the chaser. At first I got a little agitated with him calling me all the time, but I decided I just needed time to get used to it. It was nice to be pursued for once and to experience what it was like for a guy to show interest in me. I figured he was the type of guy that I needed to be with, so I forced myself to like him.

After about a month of talking and hanging out, we ended up having sex, and afterwards things about him started to get on my nerves. I started avoiding his calls, and when I did talk to him our conversations were brief. I continued to mistreat him until I finally broke the news that I didn't think he and I should talk anymore. I felt bad because he was a nice guy, but I just didn't think he was the right guy for me. After breaking up, we lost contact for a few years but later reconnected and developed a long-distance friendship.

Throughout the friendship, Jeff and I talked over the phone periodically and became a support and sounding board for one another. We shared relationship stories and advice from the male and female perspective. Since Devin, I hadn't really found a guy I could connect with, but I always felt comfortable talking to Jeff because it seemed like he really understood me. At times during our friendship, I would get mad and cut communication with him if he said something I didn't like, but he never held it against me. When I got over what I was mad about and initiated communication again, he never threw it back in my face. We just picked up where we had left off and continued the friendship. I liked that about him. He was one of the few people I felt I could be my real self around without being judged or rejected. He always accepted me just as I was.

While William and I were together, I sometimes vented to Jeff about my frustrations and desires for the relationship. Jeff listened and repeatedly expressed that he didn't think William was the one for me. He would try to give me a male's perspective to convince me that the things William did weren't normal, but at the time, I didn't want to hear it. I argued that Jeff didn't know what he was talking about because I was still holding on to the fantasy that William was "the one." Ms. Wholeness, I can be stubborn sometimes, so when my mind is made up, it's challenging to convince me otherwise. Jeff understood that about me and just let me figure it out for myself.

But when I got tired of that fantasy and ended things with William, Jeff was the first one I ran to. Since we had been friends for so long and had developed such a deep connection, I thought maybe it was meant for us to be together. Ms. Wholeness, how could I have possibly been ready to move on to someone else within days of breaking up with the man I had wanted to marry and spend the rest of my life with? At the time, I justified my behavior by thinking that William and I didn't really have a relationship anyway. I convinced myself that since we didn't spend a lot of time together or communicate much, the relationship had actually been over a long time ago and I didn't need that much time to heal. In my mind, there was nothing to heal from. Sounds silly, right? Well, at the time that was my truth and reasoning for jumping head over heels for Jeff.

Jeff lived in Florida, and I was still in Maryland, but we talked for hours on the phone at night and would text-message each other throughout the day. Jeff was a Christian, a skilled barber, and part owner of an organization that served youth. He was also attentive, expressive, romantic, and understanding—which satisfied everything I thought I had lacked with William. I rationalized that since Jeff lived in Florida, I would still have time to spend by myself to heal, so it was okay to be his friend and communicate. It's funny how we can rationalize our way into doing the very thing that isn't healthy for us. I recognize now that I was desperately seeking an object of affection to distract me from all the unresolved emotions lying dormant within me. However, I didn't see it that way then. I felt deserving of all that Jeff was giving me and that I was finally looking out for myself. Deep down, I still cared about William and how he felt, but I suppressed those emotions whenever they surfaced so I could continue focusing on me. It seemed like the right thing to do.

Only four days after breaking up with William, I reached the conclusion that Jeff was my Boaz (from Ruth, chapter 2, in the Bible), the one I had been waiting for. Once I came to that conclusion, things progressed rather quickly. In my mind, we had been friends for so long that it made sense to be together. On the other hand, it had been at least three years since we'd seen each other in person, and the last time I had seen him, I wasn't attracted to him at all. So to confirm our connection, I needed to see him again.

I went to visit him about a month after we went back to talking frequently. I prayed and asked God that if Jeff was the one for me, to turn my attractions toward him. When I landed at the airport in Florida and was on my way down the escalator to baggage claim, I saw Jeff standing there waiting for me, and instantly, I felt an attraction to him. That seemingly answered prayer was all I needed to continue going full speed ahead into this relationship, while ignoring the caution signs flashing before my eyes.

What sort of warning signs? For starters, Jeff was just getting back on his feet after moving back from California, where he had abruptly broken up with his fiancée, whom he'd been living with. Secondly, he didn't have a valid driver's license, so I had to drive him everywhere while I was visiting. He also didn't have enough money to buy me dinner, so I had to pay for everything. And finally, we were too intimate with one another too soon, which tempted me to want to have sex even though I was abstaining.

At the time, none of those things mattered to me. I was intoxicated by the way Jeff made me feel. My weekend in Florida had been just what I needed it to be emotionally, so when I got back home I was floating and ready to introduce him to my close friends and family. A few weeks later, we arranged for him to come to Maryland. A good friend of mine was having a birthday party for her husband, so I figured that would be a prime opportunity for some of my close friends to meet him and let me know what they thought. Yes, I was bringing him around my people to see what they thought about him, but in actuality, my mind was already made up. Jeff was a charmer, so he impressed my friends and received their stamp of approval. They knew how unhappy I had been with William, so their main concern was my happiness.

I also took Jeff to meet two couples from my old church who had welcomed me into their family when I moved to the DC metro area. They had both been married for over twenty years, so I valued their opinion and wanted their blessing of Jeff. Both couples seemed to like him, so I felt like I had done my due diligence.

Everything was lining up the way I wanted, so after Jeff went back home, he and I began to discuss marriage. Eager to see each other again, I planned a trip to visit him over Christmas. One day as we were discussing marriage, I asked what he thought about us getting married when I came for Christmas. He was cool with that, so we made plans to get married on New Year's Eve. No proposal. No engagement period. No ring from him (I purchased it myself). Just a casual conversation that sounded more like a business venture than a marriage. My desire was to take premarital classes so we could talk through things before getting married, but our long-distance relationship complicated that. Being the researcher that I am, I found an online class where we could watch a video together and fill out a booklet. We were basically going through the motions because we felt like we already knew each other. In my eyes, we were the perfect combination.

When I shared the news about Jeff and me deciding to get married, many people were shocked. But they were happy for me at the same time. Some questioned why I was moving so hastily and asked if I was sure, but I had received the "signs from God" that I was looking for and was determined to get married. Not only was my decision driven by my emotions and sense of lack, but a few years before that I had written in my journal that God had said I would be married by 2009. Well, the year was abruptly coming to an end, and my relationship with William hadn't ended in marriage like I wanted, so Jeff had to be the one. I thought for sure that this was God's desire for me. Ms. Wholeness, it's funny how we use God to justify our decisions even though they aren't wise or logical.

So, on December 31, 2009, in the presence of a few of my family members, I married the man I thought I would spend the rest of my life with. After the wedding, we packed up his apartment and rented a truck, and I drove all the way back to Maryland with my new husband, thinking the rest would be "happily ever after." It would prove to be anything but that.

The first year of our marriage seemed to go smoothly. We settled into the condo I was living in, and he found a job shortly after. We attended church together, he started getting involved in ministry, we joined a newlywed ministry, and we traveled and seemed to be really enjoying each other. During that time I finished writing my first book, *Living for Today: Inspirations for the Soul,* and started the process of publishing. I had already fantasized that we were going to be the example of how to have a healthy marriage. But that fantasy proved short-lived as we ventured into our second year of marriage.

In February of 2011, Jeff lost his job and had a difficult time finding work because he didn't have a degree. Despite his talents as a barber, he didn't have a license, so I suggested he go to school to get his license. The program would take about a year and seemed the logical choice. But Jeff wasn't really fond of that idea and suggested he build his own music management company instead. He had been working in the music industry for a long time while in Florida, so he had an eye and ear for talent. By this time I had published my book, so I figured he could be my manager and help me promote it as a way to generate more income for us.

Wanting to be a supportive wife, I went along with Jeff's business venture, but things didn't seem to come together. I started to notice things about Jeff and to realize he wasn't the guy who had it all together like I had thought. I started seeing his character flaws, impulses, and lack of direction and wisdom—a vast difference from the strategic, established, wise man William had been. The blinders I had been wearing were starting to come off, and I felt uncertain about how to handle it all. Yet, I kept my feelings to myself and acted as if everything was okay. I was wearing a mask for fear of others finding out that I had made a mistake.

Months went by. Jeff had no success finding a job, and I started to feel the strain of just one income. I was the sole breadwinner and the one we agreed would manage the money, so I was constantly monitoring our accounts to make sure we could pay our bills. Jeff was a spender, so he often thought of things that he needed money for, but didn't seem to be working as hard to find ways to make money. That bothered me. Although I didn't have an emotional connection with my stepfather, he had always done whatever he had to do to find and keep a job, so I wasn't used to living with a man who didn't work. Ms. Wholeness, I was trying to be empathetic, but I was also judging him for not working hard enough to find another job.

Jeff's job situation was also making him very depressed, so I spent a lot of days encouraging and reassuring him that things would get better. Things continued to move slowly, so one day Jeff decided that his music business would pick up if he moved back to Florida for a few months to get things together. He said all of his music connections were down there, so he would need to go there to get the business established. What?? How in the world would living apart be the solution for a newlywed couple? I had never heard of a married couple living apart from one another for an extended period of time, so I wasn't fond of the idea. But at the same time, I didn't want to get in the way of his endeavors, so I reluctantly agreed to him staying in Florida for a few months to get his music management business in order. While he was away, we talked frequently and agreed that he would come home at least once a month. This, however, added to our financial strain.

One of the reasons I had chosen to marry Jeff was that I thought he would shower me with attention and cure my loneliness. What I didn't realize was that I would end up being married, but still feeling alone. As we spent more time apart, it appeared Jeff was growing comfortable in Florida and didn't have any definitive plans for coming back to Maryland. As Thanksgiving and Christmas approached, Jeff made an excuse about needing to stay in Florida instead of spending the holidays with me. I was heartbroken. I felt foolish as I explained to my family and friends why Jeff and I were spending this time apart. I continued to put up the front that I was strong and was just being a supportive wife, but inside I was in so much pain.

After much pleading from me, Jeff eventually came back to Maryland, but he seemed miserable. I tried my best to comfort and encourage him, but it just didn't seem to be enough. By 2012, our marriage seemed to be on life support, but all the while, I was still painting the image that everything was okay. I wasn't willing to face the reality of what was happening and how unhappy I was, so I buried it deep within. We were supposed to work out. We were supposed to be different from other couples. But it seemed we were becoming just like everyone else—a couple in desperate need of help.

My friends voiced their concerns to me about the marriage and what they saw, but I reassured them that everything was fine and we were just going through a rough season. But on October 6, 2012, I could no longer hide the truth from my friends. I was completely exposed and looking at the broken pieces of my life that had shattered before my eyes. Now what?

I was devastated to learn that Jeff had packed all of his things and left, but I was still willing to try to make it work. For ten months I prayed, fasted, and waited for my husband to come back home. We talked about him moving back to Maryland once he got himself together, but he never gave me a definitive answer. I relied heavily on scriptures to help me to heal. Psalm 91 became the scripture I meditated on constantly. I specifically clung to the words of verses 1–2: "Those who live in the shelter of the Most High will find rest in the shadow of the Almighty. This I declare about the Lord: He alone is my refuge, my place of safety; he is my God, and I trust him." I needed to abide under the protection of God and trust Him for guidance because I had no idea what to do.

As time went by and I had space to be with myself to pray and process everything that had happened, I started to feel like what I was going through in my marriage was the result of my sin of moving ahead of God and marrying Jeff instead of waiting on Him. I had run to Jeff for comfort to fill my emotional void, and as a result I married a man who left his home to "find himself" and chose to follow his passion for music instead of honoring his vows and taking care of his wife. I married a man who said he was a Christian and submitted to God, but it seemed like he was more submitted to his own agenda, which led to him not being able to fully commit to me. I thought I had been listening to God, but in reality I was listening to me.

A dark cloud loomed over me as I started to feel the ache and pain of facing the truth. Then anger settled in. I was angry at Jeff for doing this to me. And deep down inside, I was angry with myself for choosing him. I never thought he would hurt me. I didn't realize how broken I was and that he was broken too. In the midst of it all, I felt God telling me to be still and let Him work it out because I had done all I knew to do. And daily, God sent words of encouragement through someone sending an email, scriptures from the Bible, or whispers from the Holy Spirit inside of me that seemed to speak directly to me. Ms. Wholeness, I was experiencing a vicious storm, but God was seeing me through.

However, on August 18, 2013, I received more news adding to an already devastating situation. A woman on my social media page wrote that she and Jeff were engaged and living together. My heart sank. Thankfully, I was hanging out with friends that day, so they were there to comfort me and tell me what to do next. To avoid confrontation, I quickly blocked the woman from my page while one of my friends went into investigation mode to find out more details. She quickly discovered the woman's page on another social media site, including several pictures of her and Jeff together.

As I looked at my husband and this other woman together, everything around me stood still. My body felt numb. Shock and disbelief left me emotionless. I had never suspected Jeff was cheating on me. I felt embarrassed and like such a big fool.

I took a screen shot of the photos and sent them to Jeff via text, demanding answers. When he didn't respond to my text, I called repeatedly, but he wouldn't answer. I called his mentor to tell him about what I had found out, and he said he would talk to him and asked me to give him time. It took days—days that felt like years as I waited in agony to learn when, how, and why Jeff had done this.

Eventually, Jeff admitted to the affair and answered my many questions. I was willing to stay with him and thought that if he came home, we could go to counseling and work through it. However, despite my attempts to stay together, Jeff felt he had messed up too much and that it would be best for us to get a divorce. He felt like he didn't want to put in the work to restore our marriage. I felt abandoned and rejected, not worthy to be chosen or to be number one, a first priority.

My marriage was over. Not only did I have to let go of all the hope I was holding onto and adjust to a new normal; I also had to schedule a doctor's appointment for an STD test. In my promiscuous days, I had contracted five STDs. All were curable except one: herpes. As a result, I hated getting STD tests taken, for fear that I had contracted something deadly. But now my husband's infidelity triggered this fear. How in the world had I ended up here?

Prior to finding out about Jeff's infidelity, I had made an appointment for us to see a Christian counselor. After Jeff had agreed to go to counseling, I had booked a flight for him to come home. I had specifically looked for a male counselor who could identify with Jeff and understand his perspective. After finding out about the other woman, I cancelled his flight but kept the counseling appointment for myself. The timing was perfect for helping me navigate my next steps. I needed to understand how I had ended up in this situation so I could prevent myself from making the same mistakes again. I didn't trust myself when it came to choosing a man. I needed help because I had made too many wrong choices in the past to know what a healthy relationship looked like. I felt confused and wondered if I could really hear God speaking to me because I thought He had spoken to me about these men, but I was wrong. I had become discouraged in discerning the voice of God and wondered if I was reading and hearing things based only on what I wanted. The cycle of unhealthy relationships needed to stop. All hell had broken loose, and I had reached my breaking point.

Questions for reflection:

- Have you ever been in a relationship with someone you knew wasn't good for you? What made you stay?

- Have you ever been so determined to have something (e.g., a husband, kids) that you ignored everything and everybody to get it? What was the outcome?

- When have you worn a mask around others to hide what was going on with you? Have you taken that mask off? If so, what motivated you to remove it? If not, what keeps you wearing that mask? Are you willing to remove it now?

- Based on your responses, what do you notice that is still unresolved? What actions will you take to start your journey of healing in this area?

Seven

How Do I Deal with This Pain?

During my first counseling session, I knew I had chosen the right counselor. After I gave him a brief synopsis of what had happened in my marriage, he responded with understanding. He quickly picked up on the fact that I didn't love or take care of myself but rather looked for others to make me feel loved, wanted, and worthy. Ouch! He also discerned the trust issues I had and explained how they were showing up in my relationships. A deeper level of healing had begun.

One of the first things we discussed was accepting responsibility for the part that I played in my marriage falling apart. I accepted the responsibility of moving hastily into marriage without healing from my previous relationships. I also accepted the responsibility of thinking I knew what was best for me and not taking time to seek wise counsel and really hear from God. I accepted the responsibility for being led by my emotions and looking for a man to make me whole, instead of looking to God. I accepted the truth that I had to deal with the consequences of my decisions and seek healing so that I could walk in wholeness.

Ms. Wholeness, it was so easy for me to play victim and blame my ex-husband for all he had done to me. But in order to heal, I had to face the part I played in it too. Facing the truth is painful because it requires humility in admitting that I'm imperfect and have flaws too. After leaving my first counseling session, I reflected on all that had taken place during my marriage and realized that it could have been worse, but God kept me. Then I reflected on Psalm 18:19, which says, "He led me to a place of safety; he rescued me because he delights in me." Through that scripture I realized that God had revealed the truth to me about Jeff and his infidelity so I wouldn't continue to hope that we would work things out. I thanked God for protecting me from continuing to give my heart, money, and body to Jeff. I felt God had rescued me from that dangerous relationship because He delights in me and loves me so much that He wanted to deliver me to safety. When the reality of all that had happened finally sank in, I sat on the floor in my bedroom and let out a painful cry. I needed to release.

From that point, all I could do was take things one day at a time. An instrumental part of my healing process was spending time with my friends. We got together regularly and shared what was going on with us. Their encouragement and support really helped me make it through the tough days.

The hardest part to deal with was at night when I lay down in the bed Jeff and I used to share. During those nights a deep, dark pain formed in my chest, and I could feel an ache in my heart. It was a reminder that he was gone and I was all alone. Facing the ugly truth hurt.

I chose to schedule weekly appointments with my counselor to help process my emotions and work through the trauma I had experienced in my marriage. One of the first things he asked me to do was make a list of my emotional needs—the things that make me feel loved in a relationship. That was something I hadn't taken the time to define for myself. I had thoughts in my head of what I needed, but it helped to write them out. I came up with eight primary needs: to be understood, listened to, paid attention to, transparent and free to express my emotions, trusted, secure, respected, and supported. When I compared that list to the people I had been in relationships with, I could see what need each was meeting at the time.

My counselor also gave me an emotions inventory list so I could begin labeling my emotions. Until this point I wasn't skilled in naming my emotions because I was preoccupied with suppressing or denying them. The only feelings I knew were "happy" and "sad." I had no idea there were primary emotions such as happiness, caring, depression, inadequacy, fear, confusion, hurt, anger, loneliness, and remorse, and that under those were a plethora of secondary emotions ranging from strong to light. My counselor encouraged me to look at the emotional vocabulary list whenever I felt something so I could start to name what I was feeling.

I had grown up around "strong" women who didn't support expressing emotions. Feelings were seen as a sign of weakness to be suppressed or discouraged. Whenever I shared how I felt, my mom would say, "Stop thinking like that" or "Don't let that get to you." Then she would quickly go to the positive, which made me think that how I felt didn't matter. My counselor helped me to understand that on some levels, I had been emotionally abandoned by my dad and my mom because I didn't have a safe space to be human and express how I felt. So my counselor created a safe environment for me to talk and share without judgment. As a result, we uncovered something I had only shared with a few people: that I had been molested by a family member when I was around five. Prior to counseling, I didn't think it was a big deal but I saw now how it had contributed to my trust issues with men and the desire to be sexually stimulated from a young age.

Ms. Wholeness, it felt great to be in counseling and to understand more of who I am. But at the same time, every emotion I had suppressed for over thirty years was now coming to the surface, and it was overwhelming. Imagine the cap of a fire hydrant coming off and water flying out everywhere. That's what it felt like to unpack the baggage in my life.

I was also being challenged to develop a new coping mechanism for my pain. For as long as I could remember, I had used men to cope with my emotions. I looked to them as a source of happiness, fulfillment, and distraction from the hatred I had for myself. Now that I was separated and choosing not to jump into another relationship, I felt the huge void of not having a man in my life. I had never been in this place before because I was always dealing with it in some way. Loneliness began to creep in, and I started longing for an object of affection.

When the longing became unbearable, I would reach out via text or social media to spark up conversations with past lovers to see if they would take the bait and give me the fix of attention that I craved. None of them ever responded the way I wanted. I would also text my ex-husband to seek his attention, but every time it proved hazardous to my emotional state. On one hand, communicating with him made me think of how much I still loved him; on the other hand, so many questions surfaced about him and the other woman.

In the past, I had been looking for a healthy relationship to attach myself to, but I never found it in the men I was with because none of them had the capacity to give me what I needed. They were all emotionally unavailable. I learned to deprive myself of what I needed because that's what I had grown up around. Talking to my ex-husband only contributed to my beliefs about being unwanted and unloved because he made it clear that he didn't desire to remain married. What really sealed it for me was when I snooped on his social media page one day and saw a post he had written about the other woman. There, he said that he wanted to be with her because she was worth it. Reading that post sent a dagger into my heart and reinforced my sense of inadequacy and of not being worthy of love. I felt like Leah, whose story is told in Genesis 29 in the Bible.

Leah was married to a man named Jacob, who was also married to her sister Rachel. Jacob loved Rachel and had desired to marry her from the beginning. However, the man who would be Jacob's father-in-law tricked him into marrying Leah first by claiming it was their custom for the firstborn to marry first. As a result of this arranged marriage, Leah spent her time trying to win her husband's love. She did this by giving of herself and bearing him children, namely sons. With the birth of each child, she thought surely that would get him to love her, but he never did. As a matter of fact, Leah died never having gained the love she desired from Jacob.

Sounds like such a sad story, right? Well, Ms. Wholeness, I can relate to how Leah felt because that's how I had been feeling. I felt like running after men who didn't want me in return was the story of my life. Several men from my past came to mind, and with each situation of rejection, I felt lower, lesser, and increasingly devalued. With all these men choosing other women over me, and the common denominator being me, I concluded that something must be wrong with me and that I wasn't good enough to be chosen. It hurt like hell to be in that space time after time. The ache I felt while exploring these emotions made me feel like I was going insane. But it was a necessary part of the healing process. My wounds had to be exposed so they could heal.

During this time my counselor encouraged me to develop boundaries to create a safe space for myself in order to heal. He gave me a visual of what those boundaries would look like. He said, "Imagine a big house with a yard and a fence around it. Outside the house is a sidewalk.

You represent that house, and you have the ability to determine whether a person stays outside the fence on the sidewalk, comes past the fence and into the yard, comes up the stairs and onto the porch, comes into the house and stands in the foyer, or goes up the stairs to the bedroom." Then he encouraged me to identify those people who were not healthy for me and for the sake of my healing so I would not allow them in my yard during this season of my life.

I identified a couple of men as unsafe because I had been reaching out to them in my moments of weakness. They weren't bad people—just not healthy for my growth. I also decided to limit the activities I was involved in so I wouldn't distract myself with busyness, which was another way of neglecting myself. I had to create a safe space to heal. I also limited my social media use because it was creating a doorway for guys from my past to access me. I wasn't at a point where I could close my social media sites completely, so I took breaks from the sites to spend time with myself.

I remember an episode of *Iyanla, Fix My Life* where she said daughters marry their fathers. That's exactly what I had done. When I was growing up, my dad wasn't emotionally or physically available. All he ever really gave me were words filled with promises he couldn't keep. Since I was used to just receiving words without action, that's what I looked for a man to give me. I saw the similarities between my dad and my ex-husband, which helped me understand what had contributed to my choosing him. Jeff was skilled in feeding me the words I liked to hear, just like my dad had been. My dad was financially unstable, and so was Jeff. My dad wasn't physically there; Jeff wasn't either. My dad abandoned his responsibility of being a father, and Jeff abandoned the role of being a husband. Another correlation I discovered was how my first love experience had caused my understanding of love to get distorted. Typically a father provides the emotional stimulation for his daughter by hugging, kissing, and affirming her in a nonsexual way, so that sets the example for a male relationship. Well, Ms. Wholeness, since my first valuable male relationship was with Devin, and included emotional and sexual interaction, the wires got crossed in my learning about how a man should treat a woman. I realized that our breakup was a severe form of rejection because Devin was my first example of love and acceptance from a man. I had been molested by my great-uncle, was abandoned by my father, and didn't get along with my stepfather, so when I met Devin, he set the standard—including the introduction of sensuality in a relationship. That's why it's so important for a daughter to experience her father's love before becoming involved with a man on a sexual level.

At this time my dad and I were on better terms than we had been in the past, but after I had realized all these things about my connection with men, I became angry with him whenever he said "I love you, baby." To me, they were just words, which I felt had contributed to my low expectations of men. I didn't want to tell him how I felt because we had already had several conversations about my painful feelings toward him and had finally reached the point of being able to communicate more consistently. I didn't want to keep holding the past over his head; however, every time he sent a text saying "I love you," I felt triggered. So I finally generated the courage to tell him how I felt and called him on the phone. As I expressed my feelings, he was quiet. Then he apologized for making me feel that way, but he also said he wondered how long I would hold what he had done over his head.

He was right. I couldn't keep blaming him for the decisions I had made. I needed to take responsibility for my own actions. It took time for me to release those feelings toward my dad. I talked with my counselor about it, wrote in my journal, and prayed for God to help me to accept that my dad hadn't had the capacity to be the man that I needed him to be. He didn't grow up with a father in his life, so he had done the best he could with what he had. He later told me that he knew my mom and grandmother were taking good care of me and that I would be okay. So understanding his limitations, I had to shift the focus back to me. I was so used to hiding from myself, having learned to do so at an early age. For instance, as a child, when my stepfather would have one of his fits of rage after drinking, I would mostly stay in my room and hide, checking out mentally and emotionally. That's how I learned how to cope with traumatic experiences. So after my abortions, I had gone into deeper hiding within myself, which created in me an emotional disconnect. I needed to learn how to reconnect with myself and be present to my own emotions.

Another way I had found to cope with my emotions was through masturbation, which I started after choosing not to have sex with guys. When I didn't want to face the pain of what I was feeling and didn't have a man in my life to run to, I used masturbation to self-medicate. It made me feel good for a moment and provided a sense of relief. It wasn't the act, but the endorphins, that I was running to. Although my body experienced pleasure, my soul felt guilt and condemnation because I struggled with whether masturbation was a sin. I knew I was being led by my fleshly desires and not by the Spirit of God, like the Bible teaches in Romans 8, so I was conflicted internally. But the conflict wasn't enough to make me stop. Essentially, I found ways to cope but never really gave myself permission to experience the emotions from my childhood. Because I didn't express my emotions dating back to the traumatic events of the past, I wasn't able to respond like a healthy human being.

Ms. Wholeness, it's human to cry when we feel abandoned, rejected, or threatened, yet so many of us treat our emotions as enemies. We shut them down, dismiss them, or try not to feel at all. I understand now that our emotions are like the "check engine" light in our cars—an indicator that something deeper is going on that needs our attention. We can either choose to explore ourselves to figure out what's going on, or we can just ignore it until we break down and can't function. I needed to honor my emotions to allow the little girl in me to grieve and be human.

Until counseling, I had never talked about what I had gone through as a child and had someone normalize my experience and offer understanding. For so long I felt like such a bad person, but the more I dug deep into my past and who I was, the better I understood that the traumatic experiences weren't my fault and it was okay to grieve what had happened. So acknowledging how I felt, labeling my emotions, and letting the little girl in me grieve was the pathway to reconnecting with myself. Knowing that I could change and that I didn't have to continue to live in that space gave me hope.

The awareness that there was a little girl inside of me who needed a voice really struck me, and I started to feel her existence—the poor little girl who had been locked up inside for so long, who wasn't allowed to feel or grieve, so she just went on with life as if everything was okay. That poor little deprived soul. The poor little girl within me had been trapped in a prison cell for over thirty years, being mistreated by me. I could see her sitting on a cold prison floor dressed in filthy rags. Her knees to her chest, scruffy hair and puppy-dog eyes. Sitting behind the black steel bars, waiting for someone to come along and set her free. When she cried out for help through the longing in my soul, I would reach out externally, thinking that would set her free. But all this time she had been waiting for *me* to set her free.

Finally now, my message to her was this: "Well, I'm here, little girl, to rescue you from your past. I won't let anyone else harm you. You're safe now. I'm sorry it took me so long to get to you, but I'm here now. You can be free now. You don't have to hide anymore because I will take care of you. You don't have to look to anyone for love anymore, because I will love you. You are free to live now, little girl. The past is gone and the pain is no more."

I felt so sorry for her, now that I understood her. She just wanted to be protected, understood, and loved. She wanted to feel wanted and like she mattered. The adults in her life had let her down and hadn't known how to give her what she needed. They failed her. That poor little girl. So innocent, sweet, pure, living in a troubled, chaotic, and unhealthy environment. She lived with two broken people who contributed to her brokenness. Understanding the little girl in me made me want to love her and let her know that it was going to be okay. I wanted to protect her, to let her know that she wouldn't ever have to feel that way again. I wanted to offer reassurance that she wasn't to blame for what had happened to her, that she is a treasure and deserves to be treated as such. All of this offered me a whole new perspective on taking care of myself. It made me want to treat the little girl inside me better because she deserves, needs, and is worthy of that type of love and care. For a long time, I had felt like the real me was trapped inside and I just needed to break free. That awakening was a breakthrough moment for me and provided a step toward acceptance. I began to embrace me.

A few days after my awakening experience, I attended a women's sister circle called "REAL Women," founded by Dr. Trenace Richardson, whom I had met at church. I had always felt connected to her when she preached at church because I could sense a beautiful worshipper-spirit exuding from her. I had been excited to learn she was starting a women's Bible Study. During the first session she explained that the monthly meetings would be a safe space for women to open up, share, be transparent, and express how we felt. As we each shared where we felt God was calling us, I was amazed at how many in the room had similar callings, struggles, and experiences. Several women spoke about feeling called to minister to broken women and shared that they were going through the healing process themselves. Several women mentioned issues of abandonment and rejection, which seemed so timely after I had just discovered that about myself in counseling. Leaving that meeting, I felt that God was ordering my steps and leading me to places that would help me to heal.

Ms. Wholeness, I wish I could tell you that things continued to go uphill and I never experienced a negative emotion after those powerful moments, but I wouldn't be telling the truth. I learned that the reality of the healing process is that it is filled with ups and downs. Some days will be peaceful and full of contentment, and other days you may feel like you're going insane. For me, it felt like a tug-of-war between the old and the new me, so I had to endure the process. The old me was used to being with a man and just wanted to go on a date and have a guy pay attention to me; I wanted the opportunity to meet the "right" man. But the new me said I may as well stop looking because "Mr. Right" wasn't coming right now; I wasn't ready, and I needed this time to heal and reconnect with me. My flesh longed for the familiar, but I was learning how to starve those unhealthy desires and adopt new ways of being. I was learning to break my addiction and adjust to the new normal of life without a man. No more business as usual; I was determined to make a lifestyle change.

I realized that the healing process would not happen overnight, although I really wished it would! At times I felt broken, sad, incapacitated, and paralyzed. Some days I didn't want to do anything but sit and sulk. I started thinking about my friends who had been single for years, and cringed at the thought of a long period of singleness. Who was I without a man? What was I really worth? Ms. Wholeness, I didn't know the answer, but I was determined to find out.

I needed to allow my heart to break, to give myself permission to feel the pain and grieve so many losses: my marriage, my last name, the years I had spent in the marriage, the happiness I had expected in marriage, the chance to have children with Jeff, my dignity, my testimony of a healthy marriage, the witness of a marriage that works. I needed to grieve the loss of the life I had expected to have with Jeff, which didn't come to fruition. Allowing myself to experience this grief was another sign I was learning to offer myself acceptance.

As I went through the healing process, I found myself becoming distant in my relationship with God because I was angry with Him for allowing Jeff to cheat and not allowing the marriage to work. I believed God knew how much I had prayed and waited in faith for things to turn around, but they didn't. I was angry at God for allowing this to happen to me when He could have stopped it. There were also times when I got angry and frustrated with God because He wasn't moving me through the healing process fast enough. I wanted quick answers that just wouldn't come.

One day I was so anxious and worked up that I couldn't calm down. I prayed for God to help me calm down so I could hear Him, but I couldn't seem to find that peace. I prayed, tried to quiet myself, read a scripture about being anxious, lay on the floor in the fetal position. I was doing everything I thought I needed to do to find peace, but it seemed nothing was working. In that moment Jesus wasn't enough; I wanted a man instead. I couldn't see God or hear Him talk to me in an audible voice, so I wanted a man.

Ms. Wholeness, have you ever felt like God wasn't enough? In those moments the last thing you want to hear someone say is "Trust God" or "Just spend time with Him and let Him be your man." Hearing those words set me off and made me even angrier because that wasn't what I wanted to hear. I wanted a man to hold me tight, kiss me, and whisper sweet nothings in my ear. Deep down I knew that God was the only one who could truly heal me and love me the way I needed to be loved. But I was being stubborn and prideful. I had to figure out how to connect with Him in a way that was authentic and fulfilling.

For me, it started with honesty. I grabbed my journal and frantically began to write.

> *Lord, I'm trying to get in your presence*
> *but my mind won't calm down. I know you see me*
> *trying to get to you. Why won't you reach out and*
> *grab me when you see that I'm struggling? Times*
> *like this are when I want to say just forget it! It's*

too hard trying to get into your presence. It's been 30

minutes and I'm still not at peace. GOD, I NEED

PEACE! GIVE ME YOUR PEACE RIGHT

NOW! WHY ARE YOU IGNORING ME?

WHY WON'T YOU HELP ME? YOU SEE

I'M STRUGGLING RIGHT NOW TO GET

IN YOUR PRESENCE. COME GET ME,

FATHER! PLEASE COME GET ME!

Ms. Wholeness, I was so busy trying to get Him to come to me, while all along, He was waiting on me to press into Him. After that journal entry I put on some worship music and just began to worship and praise Him. That is when I felt His peace.

It seemed like I was estranged from God, but throughout the process, God continued to give me little nuggets of hope and inspiration. One day when I was in Florida visiting my family, I got encouragement through the weather. When I left my mom's house it was a little cloudy, but the sun was still out. As I drove out of her subdivision, it started to drizzle. Then as I drove to another part of town, the rain started to fall more heavily. Once I got to my god-sister's house, it was pouring. After I picked her up, we drove to get something to eat and it started raining so hard it was difficult to see where we were going. I had to slow down in order to drive safely. When we got to the restaurant the rain had slacked off, and by the time we got back to my mom's house, the skies were clear and it looked like it had never rained. It was so amazing how there could be a drenching downpour on one side of town and little to no rain on another side of town. Then it dawned on me—that is how it is in our lives too. Sometimes the rain of life's circumstances is pouring so hard that the way ahead looks blurry and dreary. Other times our lives are filled with rays of sunshine and beautiful blessings. Throughout the weather changes, we just have to keep going and keep pushing forward, no matter what it looks like. At some point the rain has to stop and the sun has to shine. I just needed to endure until my sunny days came. I needed to slow down, stay focused on God and His words of encouragement and instructions for me, and trust that it would get better.

Questions for reflection:

- What is your current view of counseling? What has shaped that view? If you've never gone to counseling, would you consider it in the future? Why or why not?

- What are your emotional needs?

- What past, unhealthy relationship choices are you willing to acknowledge and own? What was going on within you when you made those choices?

- What lessons have you learned about yourself from your relationship experiences?

- How will you use the lessons you've learned from relationships to help others?

- Based on your responses, what do you notice that is still unresolved? What actions will you take to start your journey of healing in this area?

Eight
Can I Be Made New?

Walking in wholeness and doing the work to heal from my past issues caused me to develop a true love relationship with myself. I was flipping through old journal entries just to see how much I'd grown, and I found a letter I wrote to myself on Valentine's Day of 2014. It made me smile to see my words:

> *Dear Shavon,*
>
> *I love you. You're special to me. I know I don't always show it, but I do love you. I want to be with you. I want to treat you with the honor and respect that you deserve. You are worthy of receiving love, and I want to shower it upon you. How? I really don't know, but I will learn. I want to get to know*

you and what you like to do. I want to treat you with

love so you will not accept anything less from others.

I want you to know what love looks and feels like.

I love you, Shavon. I love how petite you are. I love

how nappy your hair is. I love your glasses. I love the

imperfect spots on your face. I love your ears. I love

your pretty teeth and smile. I love your dimples. I love

how sexy you are. I love how you want to help others

develop and grow. I love how gifted and talented you

are. I love how small your hands are. I love how

you dance. I love how you care for others. I love how

much of a fighter you are. I love that no matter what,

you won't quit. I love how much you love God and

desire to please Him. I love how bold and courageous

you are. I love how successful you are. There is so

much I love about you. You're the bomb.com and I

want you to know that.

Internally things felt chaotic but overall, I was blossoming into a beautiful butterfly, ready to spread my wings and fly.

In the process of reconnecting with myself I started to think of things I wanted to do. One thing that came to mind was to get my makeup done and take some glamour shots. By this time I had cut off my long locs and was wearing a low cut to symbolize new beginnings. I felt like a cleansing needed to take place. A young lady I used to work with did my makeup, and a photographer at my current job took my photos. Ms. Wholeness, it was so much fun! It felt so good to do something for *me* that I've always wanted to do. I felt like a real model.

I also found myself thinking more about my future and how I wanted my life to be. I created vision boards with pictures and words that described where I wanted to go. I remember one day sitting and looking at my vision boards after discovering that Jeff had filed for divorce and hadn't told me. We had been communicating on a cordial, friendly basis prior to this, and then all of a sudden I received a notice in the mail from an attorney soliciting me to hire her for an open case. When I went to the Maryland website to look up my name, I saw that he had filed a petition for divorce. I felt deceived once again because he hadn't bothered to tell me in advance. As I sat and processed my thoughts, I started looking at the two vision boards I had created. My words stood out from the first vision board:

> *I realize I'm worth it. Great wife. Going forward. Boss. Leader. Power player. Comfort for the brokenhearted. Living the abundant life. Command success. Passion for people around the globe. Life-changing speaker. Women who are shaping the world. Empowering ministry. On the move. Heal the world. Unduplicated success. Kingdom business. I am a woman of power. Today take the first step toward creating change. Motivation. Worship*

that changes lives. Confident. Wealth and financial
freedom. Passion. Purpose. Essence *magazine's*
non-fiction best-sellers list. Inspiring women every
day. Faith. Break the barriers.

The words that stood out from my second vision board were just as inspiring:

Well enough alone. Reinvent yourself. Live
your best life. You are beautiful. Going forward.
Doing well. Love yourself. You are loved. You are
valuable. You are crafted with beauty and purpose.
You were put here for a reason. There is no one like
you. There is no truth in the lie that you don't matter.
Finding peace. A man that's right for you. Worth
the effort. Change. Love yourself. Put yourself first.
Rejuvenate. Confidence. Freedom. Living single.
"Will you marry me?" Radiance. Shining moments.
Inspire.

Seeing those pictures and words reminded me of where I was going and encouraged me to stay focused on that. A force inside of me was pushing me to keep going, no matter how I felt.

That force showed me visions of the business I would own, called Walking in Wholeness, through which I would speak to women all over the world. I saw glimpses of myself teaching women how to have healthy relationships, starting with themselves. I saw myself counseling and inspiring women everywhere. Because of what I was going through, I had a passion to help women realize who they are so they can understand that they don't have to settle. I saw a vision of myself helping women live with boldness, confidence, courage, value, and worth, without needing a man in an unhealthy way. It became clear to me that I had been born to help women break free from negative perspectives of themselves. I was tired of us women being defeated, operating below our potential, and letting the sense of emptiness inside us run our lives! Then I was reminded of Isaiah 61:1 as a confirmation scripture for what I felt God was calling me to do: "He has sent me to comfort the brokenhearted and to proclaim that captives will be released and prisoners will be freed." My calling was to women who felt broken, and my very first client was me!

This explains why I was so determined and passionate to break free from the unhealthy relationship cycle I had continuously found myself in. My passion and life-calling compelled me to get free and stay free so I could fulfill the works God had created me to do. Seeing myself and other women get free excited me and fueled an incredible passion within me, which was how I knew it was what I had been born to do.

Now that my path was clear, it was imperative that I continue on my journey of healing, no matter the circumstance. So in June 2014, I started writing a blog about my process at www.shavoncarter.com. The details of my purpose were illuminated right in the middle of my pain. Isn't that something, Ms. Wholeness? When it felt like I was about to lose my footing and fall off the deep end emotionally, God strategically revealed to me why I was going through all of this and why I needed to keep moving forward. There was purpose in my pain, and He was orchestrating it so it could work for my good and His glory. What an amazing God!

Ms. Wholeness, I was growing comfortable in my own skin, so I started taking myself out on dates and doing things that I wanted to do. I took myself out to the movies, out to eat, shopping, to get ice cream, and on a weekend getaway in the mountains. I just enjoyed my own company. When I started going on intentional dates with myself, I noticed emotions surfacing. I felt unwanted when no one tried to flirt or talk to me. I felt unattractive because of my low, natural hair. When I went out, it seemed like everyone had a mate, which made me feel so alone. Then I started to wonder what I was having a "Me Date" for if I wanted to be with a guy and not alone. Maybe it was better off just staying in the house. Ms. Wholeness, it was rough in the beginning because I was in the process of shifting my thinking about being with myself and not having a man in my life. But I didn't let that stop me.

I exercised patience with myself and relaxed my expectations that I needed to feel a certain way by a certain time. And the more I did it, the more fun I had and the more I started to enjoy my own company. My goal was to learn to be kind to me and offer acceptance to myself. As time went on, I saw myself doing that more and more.

A new me was emerging, so I was glad when the day finally came for my final divorce hearing. I was ready to shed everything connected to the old me, including my married name. When I woke up that morning,

I heard the words from Psalm 73:26: "My health may fail, and my spirit may grow weak, but God remains the strength of my heart; he is mine forever." I felt those were God's words of encouragement to me as I went to court to finalize the divorce. God knew that my heart had failed and was hurting from what had happened in my marriage. God knew that I had made the wrong decision in choosing to marry Jeff. But God promised to strengthen my heart.

My close friend Tasha went with me, and a friend from church met us there. The process went smoothly, and I received the proposed order for absolute divorce before leaving the courtroom. It was over, and I felt relieved and moved to tears. Not only did I have a new beginning, but I also went back to my maiden name. Restoration! I was no longer bound by the pain attached to my old name and my old life. I was set free, and it was time to begin again. It felt good not to be in the limbo of the yearlong waiting period of separation that the state of Maryland requires. Now what? I felt the need to celebrate.

My desire to celebrate sparked the idea of having a New Beginnings party. Some people may call it a divorce party, but that's not what it represented for me. I didn't want to celebrate what I had lost but to focus on what I had gained and learned through the process. I wanted to celebrate my newfound freedom and those who had journeyed with me through the separation and divorce process. So I invited the women who were close to me and instrumental in supporting me during my transition from marriage back to the single life. These women had lent their listening ears so I could vent my frustrations. They lent me their shoulders to cry on. They held me up with their encouraging words and presence. They had done so much for me, and I wanted to give back to them.

I reserved a private room at a nice restaurant for the dinner party. We ate, laughed, danced, and had a good time celebrating my fresh start. During the party, I shared with the ladies my personal testimony of what I had gone through and what God had done for me, and encouraged them to allow Him to work in their lives too. Some of my friends got up to speak and shared beautiful words about me, such as how much I'd inspired and encouraged them as I journeyed through my process. I found it so encouraging to hear these kind words from the women who had helped me through rough times. I was thankful to share a moment not only to celebrate me but to celebrate them and the part they had played in my life.

Now that I was divorced and ready to move forward, I needed help navigating uncharted territory into my future. I realized that in order to make the transition into doing what I love, I needed to ask for help. I felt I was stuck in a rut and not moving toward my dreams, so I reached out to a life coach for the extra push I needed. I was afraid at first, but it's been the best decision of my life.

Ms. Wholeness, imagine someone walking alongside you every week, helping you unlock your potential to transform into a greater, more powerful you. My counselor had helped me unlock my past and learn more about myself. Working with a life coach helped me see my future and the endless possibilities ahead. One of the first exercises we did helped me discover who I was when I was being my authentic self. Through this exercise I learned that I am Serenity, Solace, Brilliance, Delight, and Love. This is how I show up in the world.

When my coach first read those words to me, the one that stood out the most was *Brilliance* because I had never seen myself in that way before. But it was true! I was discovering so many amazing things about me! Hiring a life coach was one of the best investments I've ever made in myself.

As I really started to work on me and the goals I wanted to accomplish, I decided the status quo was no longer acceptable. I was breaking up habits and thought processes I had been accustomed to all my life. Instead of doing things when I felt like it, I was learning how to commit to what I said I would do, whether I felt like it or not. I was starting to believe in what I can do instead of doubting myself. As you can imagine, Ms. Wholeness, it felt like another war was going on within me. I was transforming, but a part of me was still fighting to remain the same. Although I've never given birth to children of my own, I felt like I was in the birthing process. I was in labor, birthing a new me. Every challenge and pain I experienced in the transformation process was worth it. A bigger, brighter, bolder, fearless, courageous me was emerging, so I needed to continue to push.

One of the things my coach challenged me to do was something so outrageous and bold that the old me would never have done it. I wanted to break free and out of my shell, so I decided to go skydiving! I have always been afraid of heights, so I never considered jumping out of an airplane . . . until I found the courage to face my fears. Once I set my mind on it, I scheduled the appointment so I wouldn't talk myself out of it.

The closer it got to the date, the more nervous I became. One morning I woke up at three a.m. thinking about my upcoming adventure. I started feeling fearful and wondered what I was getting myself into. Then I prayed, and God reminded me that fear is really "False Evidence Appearing Real." That calmed me. Then this question, which I believe was from God, came to my mind: "How would you be if you knew nothing bad was going to happen?" I thought about it for a moment and realized I would be relaxed and would enjoy the experience. I would trust that God's angels would catch me and wouldn't let any harm come upon me. That's exactly how God wanted me to be in this experience. He was saying, "I have you. Just fly, my dove. Fly!"

After that moment, the fear left and never returned. The day came for me to go skydiving, and it was simply amazing! God gave me such a peace beyond my own understanding. How in the world could someone who was afraid of heights not even be nervous jumping from an airplane? Nobody but God could make that happen! I was so proud of myself for conquering my fear in such a huge way. The free fall was fast, but when the instructor pulled the parachute, it was like we were standing still in mid-air. Everything got quiet and still, and it felt like I was with God.

After going skydiving I felt courageous, bold, confident, and like I could do anything. Through my skydiving adventure I felt God saying, "You are amazing, Shavon! That experience revealed what I put inside of you. Remember this moment. I am with you even until the end of the earth. I will take care of you. I will protect you. When you put your trust in Me, you will not fall. My right hand will uphold you. I will sustain you. Continue to trust Me, and I will show you things you never thought possible. Eyes have not seen nor have ears heard, neither has it entered into the hearts of man what I have in store for you. Just trust Me."

Wow! What an amazing experience exposing me to the endless possibilities I had to look forward to! I had entered a new chapter of my life. This was just the beginning!

Questions for reflection:

- What do you love about yourself?

- What purpose have you found from your pain?

- What are some things that you've always wanted to do but haven't done? What's in the way of you doing those things? What steps will you take to pursue those goals?

- Based on your responses, what do you notice that is still unresolved? What actions will you take to start your journey of healing in this area?

Nine

Now What?

Why did I download ten chapters of my personal business in this book? Why would I be so transparent with someone I don't even know? Why would I relive the painful memories of my past and share them with you? Ms. Wholeness, I did it for you. If anything that I've written resonated with you, that's why I wrote it. I don't believe I went through all of that pain and healing to keep it to myself. The Bible says in Revelation 12:11, "And they overcame him by the blood of the Lamb and by the word of their testimony . . ." I would be doing God and you a disservice if I didn't share the beauty that has emerged from the ashes in my life. I needed you to know that you're not alone. I needed to be honest and share the challenges of my journey, even as a Christian. I wanted you to see that your past pain can become your purpose. I wanted you to see what faith in God can do.

Ms. Wholeness, loving yourself and seeing yourself as whole and new is possible. You don't have to be bound by what you've done or what others have done to you. Your journey won't be perfect. But it's possible to see yourself growing and maturing. Sure, even as you progress you will do things that make you think you're still the same, but you're not. Even as I write this book, I'm still learning how to be in a healthy relationship. But I'm learning that I don't have to be an expert in relationships; I'm modeling the *process*. I see my growth and I'm thankful for everything I go through. It's all a lesson to teach us something about ourselves and others.

Each day you learn something new that sheds more light on who you are. Believe that. It serves no benefit to sit and meditate on all your flaws and shortcomings. You're human, so you will have them. But so much is good and right about you outside of any flaws. Thinking on those things will be more productive and bear more fruit than dwelling on your failings. Finally, I want to leave you with four key points as you walk in wholeness:

Be honest with yourself.

Accept support from others.

Trust God with your life.

Be kind to you.

Let's take a closer look at each of these.

Be Honest with Yourself

This is the number one point I want to stress. I've experienced so much hiding from others in my life simply because I was hiding from myself and didn't want to be real about what I was feeling or experiencing. Honesty means admitting where you are without excuse or justification. It's admitting your raw truth. If you feel yourself wanting to withhold information from people about your relationship or about what's going on with you, it's probably because there's a truth within that you don't want to face. If you're in a relationship with someone that you know doesn't align with what you say you want, be honest about it. A lot of times we are dishonest with ourselves and others because we fear judgment. We wonder, "What will they say or think about me if I admit the truth?" Ms. Wholeness, the truth is that when we're in that mode of thinking, we're projecting what we think about ourselves onto others. We're really judging ourselves for knowing we're in something we don't want to be in. But we stay and settle for fear of being alone, or out of familiarity, habit, or the deep desire to be loved and wanted. When we're not honest with ourselves, we miss out on the opportunity to figure out what motivates us to go farther than we want to go and stay longer than we want to stay. The truth hurts, but it's also healing.

Accept Support from Others

Ms. Wholeness, there's nothing like having girlfriends to journey through life with. There's no way I could have made it through the dark times in my life without support from other women. I'll admit there was a time when I thought I could make it alone. Growing up as an only child, I was used to isolating and dealing with things by myself. So from my childhood years all the way through my marriage, I limited how much I shared about myself and my relationships. I know that contributed to a lot of the loneliness and emotional turmoil I experienced in past relationships. But when my ex-husband left, I chose to take a risk and open myself up to trust my friends to be there for me. When I did that, God showed me that I had a great support system, including my friend Tasha, who had recently gone through a divorce and helped me process my emotions. Our friendship grew stronger, and we learned how closely connected our purposes were. We became sisters in ministry and prayer partners.

While I was on travel in Hawaii for work, God sent me another lady who was also divorced. I met her in the lobby of the hotel where we were staying. She was on a solo vacation, and when we started talking, we connected instantly. We ended up going shopping together that day, and I shared with her what I was going through in my marriage. At that time my ex-husband and I were separated but still communicating, so I shared with her the emotions I was dealing with concerning that. She was also a Christian, so she ministered to me, shared her own personal testimony, and gave me the push I needed to stop communicating with him so I could care for my own emotions. We exchanged phone numbers during the trip, and afterwards she texted and called me periodically to check on me and give me encouraging words.

I'm thankful for my circle of girlfriends to laugh, cry, eat, and travel with. They let me know that I'm not alone in my journey and that they will be there for me, whatever I go through. Opening myself up to receive support from other women has resulted in my leading a women's small-group Bible Study once a month, starting my own relationship small group called "Against the Current," and being a lead facilitator of the "REAL Women" sister circle. Yes, in all these ways I get support from women to help me along my journey. And as a result of the women pouring goodness into me, I'm able to pour goodness into the lives of my friends and other women as well.

Ms. Wholeness, I don't know what support from women will look like for you, but I encourage you to be open to receive. Don't buy into the myth that women can't get along. Women are not perfect, but we aren't all catty, backbiting, jealous, or bitter like the media would have us believe. There are a lot of positive, Godly, supportive, and loving women out there whom God wants to bring together to support and build up one another. Be open to the women He places in your path to journey with you.

Trust God with Your Life

You may have heard people say, "Trust God," but what does that really mean? For me it has been a process of relinquishing control and understanding that my Heavenly Father is not like my earthly father. The constant has been me pursuing a relationship with Him. I continue to pray and talk to Him about what I'm going through. I continue to go to church and be involved in ministry. I continue to read and apply the scriptures to my life. The more I understand how loving, forgiving, merciful, kind, and purposeful God is, the more I can relax in knowing that He has everything under control.

Again, trusting God has been a *process* for me. My favorite scripture about trusting God is Proverbs 3:5-6: "Trust in the Lord with all your heart; do not depend on your own understanding. Seek his will in all you do, and he will show you which path to take." The words that especially speak to me from these verses are "do not depend on your own understanding." My curious and analytical mind is notorious for trying to figure things out on my own. I want to know the details about everything. But worrying about how things will turn out hasn't been working for me, so I'm choosing daily to depend on God more and more. That means I pray more about my situations. I tell Him the truth about where I am and what I feel. I ask for His guidance, and I'm learning how to wait for His response. Do I always get it right? Absolutely not! But with each day and each situation, I see progress as I consult Him more about my life. That creates an assurance that I'm good no matter what.

Ms. Wholeness, what does trusting God look like for you? Does how you relate to men interfere with how you relate to God? If so, I want to let you know that God is not like the men in your life. That truth may be hard to accept at first. The beauty is that God knows that you are having trouble seeing Him differently, so talk to Him about it. Tell Him you can't trust Him because of what your father or another man did to you. Tell Him that you see Him as a strict and mean God who is waiting to punish you for everything you've done. Tell Him you're afraid to let go. Tell Him your truth. He's been waiting on you to acknowledge it so He can show you who He really is. I don't know how God will do it for you, but I know He has a way of getting our attention. Just be honest with God and be open to how He reveals Himself to you.

Be Kind to You

After every session my counselor says to me, "Be kind to yourself," because he knows how hard I am on me. I expect my own perfection, so when I fall short of that (which happens with all humans), I am judgmental and condemning of myself. But what has helped me offer more kindness to myself is self-talk. I know it may sound weird, but it's helped tremendously. When I feel the judgment and condemnation arise, I say, "It's okay, Shavon. I love you and I accept you." Then I run down the list of the beautiful attributes that I love about myself. I offer what I need to myself, which makes me feel more connected within.

What has also helped is identifying the different parts of me and naming their characteristics and tendencies. Six parts make up who I am. I have given them different names to help differentiate them:

Shavon the "Businesswoman/Go-Getter": She is intelligent, accomplished, progressive, a risk taker, bold, courageous, artistic, creative. She has a tendency to try new ventures, speak publicly, teach workshops, write books, and plan for the future.

Michelle the "Counselor/Coach": She is quiet, reflective, shy, wise, reserved, submissive, sweet, kind, loving, loyal, friendly, giving, simple, and soft. She has the tendency to attend to her friends' needs, help other people, listen to people, share words of wisdom, journal, and be introspective.

Dee the "Fearful One": She is scared, cautious, closed-minded, comfortable, avoidant, and judgmental. She has a tendency to stay comfortable, be a creature of habit, overanalyze, procrastinate, compare herself to others, be moody, and protect herself from being hurt.

Nancy the "Freak": She is freaky, sensual, manipulative, impulsive, compulsive, and self-focused. She has a tendency to live for the now, go after temporary satisfaction, move fast in relationships, flirt, watch pornography, desire to feel good, spend, and live carelessly.

Boonquisha the "Ghetto One": She is loud, loves to dance, is the life of the party, talks with a Southern accent, and is boisterous and fun. She has a tendency to dance in public, drink, gossip, and curse when someone makes her mad.

Helen the "Spiritual One": She is faithful, God-fearing, prayerful, peaceful, connected, discerning, and wise. She has a tendency to read the Bible, pray for people, lead ministries, serve people, give spiritual guidance, walk by faith, and hear from God.

As you can see, Ms. Wholeness, some parts of me try to be the dominant force in my life. However, in being kind to myself, I am aware of when they show up, and I accept each one. There are days when I don't like Dee and Nancy because of their characteristics and tendencies, but denying their existence doesn't make them go away. My life wouldn't be fruitful if I allowed them to run the show, but I embrace them so I can love my whole self and not just the parts that I like. Oftentimes we are unkind to ourselves when we exhibit behavior that we don't like. But what if that part of you is acting out because it feels neglected by you? Accepting the not-so-good parts of you doesn't define who you are or condone the behavior. It's just you saying to that part of you, "I know you are a part of me and have needs. I love you, and I am choosing not to allow you to dictate my decisions because that wouldn't be beneficial in this situation." It may sound strange, and you may be thinking, "I don't want to do all of that." But knowing and accepting all of you leads to loving yourself more and reduces the tendency to engage in relationships and activities that are harmful to you emotionally, spiritually, and/or physically. Would you rather take the time to explore you or continue down the path you've been traveling? It's up to you.

Ms. Wholeness, I know you may be like me and want to rush the process of healing to get to the next phase, but I encourage you to have patience. Make up your mind that you are done with settling and trying to make things happen on your own. Enjoy the quality of life you have now, and find contentment in this current season of life. When you allow yourself time to heal and enjoy where you are, you can be better prepared for whoever the right man for you may be when he comes along. As with baking a cake, allow yourself to be fully ready before you "come out of the oven." Don't rush the process. Trust that God's timing is perfect and that the promises He has for you will be fulfilled. I urge you to just let Him finish the work.

In 1 Samuel, chapter 1, a woman named Hannah, who had a heart's desire to have children, cried out to God in great anguish and sorrow, begging Him to answer her prayers. When the prophet Eli found out what she was praying about, he said, "May the God of Israel grant the request you have asked of him." He didn't say when it would happen, but Hannah believed and went with that.

Ms. Wholeness, I don't know when your promise will come, but the best thing you can do is focus on doing your part by healing and enjoying the life God has given you and leaving the rest up to Him. It doesn't mean your journey will be spotless or that you won't make wrong turns along the way. But it does mean that you're not alone on this journey. God is right there with you to remind you that you don't have to strive for wholeness—you're already walking in it!

Questions for reflection:

- What things about you are you hiding from others? What fears do you have of exposing these things? What truths do you need to face about yourself in these areas?

- What support systems do you currently have in place? If you don't have a support system, what steps will you take to get support?

- What is in the way of you trusting God more? What can you do to increase your trust in Him?

- In what ways can you offer kindness to yourself?

- Based on your responses, what do you notice that is still unresolved? What actions will you take to start your journey of healing in this area?

- What value have you gotten from reading this book? (Email and tell me about it at walkinginwholenessinc@gmail.com. I would love to hear from you!)

The Sky's the Limit!
by Shavon Carter

I now know why the caged bird sings*
Time for me to fly and spread my wings
No more dimming my light for fear of my shine
No longer containing my inner ambition, it's my season, my time
I was confined by contexts of right or wrong
Now I'm driven by freedom and the purpose my heart longs
There's so much promise within me to be
I don't have to be anyone else, it's okay to be me
I'm finally loving the skin I'm in
And learning there's more to life than being with men
So many gifts and talents inside me to be realized
For years I walked blindly, now God has opened my eyes
My future is bright, whole and clear
No more waiting and anticipating, this is my year
I'll shine like a bright, beautiful jewel and let myself soar
No longer waiting, no longer talking, it's time to walk through God's open
doors.

* phrase based on title of Maya Angelou's book *I Know Why the Caged Bird Sings* (1969, 1997), which was in turn taken from the poem "Sympathy" by Paul Laurence Dunbar.

Afterword

I pray that after reading this book, you're encouraged to start or continue on your healing journey. I have poured out my heart in hopes that the words I shared would connect with and inspire you to be your highest and best self. As you have read, the key component in my healing journey was my relationship with God through Jesus Christ.

If you've never accepted Jesus as your Lord and personal Savior, I invite you to take advantage of this opportunity today. Romans 3:23 tells us that we have all sinned and fallen short of the glory of God. None of us are perfect, and we've all done things that don't align with God's will for our lives. However, continuing to live a sinful lifestyle apart from God only leads to death, but through Jesus, we can have eternal life (Romans 6:23). God is so merciful and loving that He didn't leave us with our sins to fend for ourselves. Romans 5:8 says that even while we were sinners, God sent

Jesus to die for our sins. That is such good news because it shows that He cared for us even in the middle of our mess!

To receive salvation, admit that you have sinned and need God to deliver you today. Then, speak out loud and believe in your heart that Jesus died and rose from the dead, and you shall be saved (Romans 10:9-10).

Ms. Wholeness, if you've made this confession of faith today and sealed this belief in your heart, you are now saved. It's just that simple. You are now a part of God's royal family and have your eternal resting place secured in heaven. If you've made this choice, I would love to hear from you and help you with your next steps. Email me at walkinginwholenessinc@gmail.com to share your story. This is the best decision you could have ever made! Congratulations, sis!

Scriptures, Sermons, and Messages That Helped Me on My Journey

When you struggle with accepting yourself

Genesis 1:27
So God created human beings in his own image. In the image of God he created them; male and female he created them.

Psalm 8:5-6
Yet you made them only a little lower than God and crowned them with glory and honor. You gave them charge of everything you made, putting all things under their authority.

Psalm 139:1-18
O Lord, you have examined my heart and know everything about me. You know when I sit down or stand up. You know my thoughts even when I'm far away. You see me when I travel and when I rest at home. You know everything I do. You know what I am going to say even before I say it, Lord. You go before me and follow me. You place your hand of blessing on my head. Such knowledge is too wonderful for me, too great for me to understand! I can never escape from your Spirit! I can never get away from your presence! If I go up to heaven, you are there; if I go down to the

grave, you are there. If I ride the wings of the morning, if I dwell by the farthest oceans, even there your hand will guide me, and your strength will support me. I could ask the darkness to hide me and the light around me to become night—but even in darkness I cannot hide from you. To you the night shines as bright as day. Darkness and light are the same to you. You made all the delicate, inner parts of my body and knit me together in my mother's womb. Thank you for making me so wonderfully complex! Your workmanship is marvelous—how well I know it. You watched me as I was being formed in utter seclusion, as I was woven together in the dark of the womb. You saw me before I was born. Every day of my life was recorded in your book. Every moment was laid out before a single day had passed. How precious are your thoughts about me, O God. They cannot be numbered! I can't even count them; they outnumber the grains of sand! And when I wake up, you are still with me!

Song of Solomon 4:7, 12
You are altogether beautiful, my darling, beautiful in every way . . .
You are my private garden, my treasure, my bride, a secluded spring, a hidden fountain.

Isaiah 43:1-7, 20
But now, O Jacob, listen to the Lord who created you. O Israel, the one who formed you says, "Do not be afraid, for I have ransomed you. I have called you by name; you are mine. When you go through deep waters, I will be with you. When you go through rivers of difficulty, you will not drown. When you walk through the fire of oppression, you will not be burned up; the flames will not consume you. For I am the Lord, your God, the Holy One of Israel, your Savior. I gave Egypt as a ransom for your freedom; I gave Ethiopia and Seba in your place. Others were given in exchange for you. I traded their lives for yours because you are precious to me. You are honored, and I love you.
"Do not be afraid, for I am with you. I will gather you and your children from east and west. I will say to the north and south, 'Bring my sons and daughters back to Israel from the distant corners of the earth. Bring all who claim me as their God, for I have made them for my glory. It was I who created them . . . The wild animals in the fields will thank me, the jackals and owls, too, for giving them water in the desert. Yes, I will make rivers in the dry wasteland so my chosen people can be refreshed."

Galatians 1:10
Obviously, I'm not trying to win the approval of people, but of God. If pleasing people were my goal, I would not be Christ's servant.

Ephesians 2:10
For we are God's masterpiece. He has created us anew in Christ Jesus, so we can do the good things he planned for us long ago.

Colossians 2:10
So you also are complete through your union with Christ, who is the head over every ruler and authority.

1 Peter 2:9
But you are not like that, for you are a chosen people. You are royal priests, a holy nation, God's very own possession. As a result, you can show others the goodness of God, for he called you out of the darkness into his wonderful light.

When you struggle to trust God

Genesis 12:1
The Lord had said to Abram, "Leave your native country, your relatives, and your father's family, and go to the land that I will show you."

Psalm 27:8, 14
My heart has heard you say, "Come and talk with me." And my heart responds, "Lord, I am coming." . . . Wait patiently for the Lord. Be brave and courageous. Yes, wait patiently for the Lord.

Proverbs 3:5-7
Trust in the Lord with all your heart; do not depend on your own understanding. Seek his will in all you do, and he will show you which path to take. Don't be impressed with your own wisdom. Instead, fear the Lord and turn away from evil.
Isaiah 40:31
But those who trust in the Lord will find new strength. They will soar high on wings like eagles. They will run and not grow weary. They will walk and not faint.

Lamentations 3:25-26
The Lord is good to those who depend on him, to those who search for him. So it is good to wait quietly for salvation from the Lord.

Colossians 2:7
Let your roots grow down into him, and let your lives be built on him. Then your faith will grow strong in the truth you were taught, and you will overflow with thankfulness.

Hebrews 11:1
Faith shows the reality of what we hope for; it is the evidence of things we cannot see.

When you need to feel secure

Genesis 19:16-17
When Lot still hesitated, the angels seized his hand and the hands of his wife and two daughters and rushed them to safety outside the city, for the Lord was merciful. When they were safely out of the city, one of the angels ordered, "Run for your lives! And don't look back or stop anywhere in the valley! Escape to the mountains, or you will be swept away!"

Exodus 13:17
When Pharaoh finally let the people go, God did not lead them along the main road that runs through Philistine territory, even though that was the shortest route to the Promised Land. God said, "If the people are faced with a battle, they might change their minds and return to Egypt."

Proverbs 4:12
When you walk, you won't be held back; when you run, you won't stumble.

Psalm 18:19
He led me to a place of safety; he rescued me because he delights in me.
Psalm 59:9, 16
You are my strength; I wait for you to rescue me, for you, O God, are my fortress . . . But as for me, I will sing about your power. Each morning I will sing with joy about your unfailing love. For you have been my refuge, a place of safety when I am in distress.

Psalm 91:1-16
Those who live in the shelter of the Most High will find rest in the shadow of the Almighty. This I declare about the Lord: He alone is my refuge, my place of safety; he is my God, and I trust him. For he will rescue you from every trap and protect you from deadly disease. He will cover you with his feathers. He will shelter you with his wings. His faithful promises are your armor and protection. Do not be afraid of the terrors of the night, nor the arrow that flies in the day. Do not dread the disease that stalks in darkness, nor the disaster that strikes at midday. Though a thousand fall at your side, though ten thousand are dying around you, these evils will not touch you. Just open your eyes, and see how the wicked are punished. If you make the Lord your refuge, if you make the Most High your shelter, no evil will conquer you; no plague will come near your home. For he will order his angels to protect you wherever you go. They will hold you up with their hands so you won't even hurt your foot on a stone. You will trample upon lions and cobras; you will crush fierce lions and serpents under your feet! The Lord says, "I will rescue those who love me. I will protect those who trust in my name. When they call on me, I will answer; I will be with them in trouble. I will rescue and honor them. I will reward them with a long life and give them my salvation."

Proverbs 1:33
But all who listen to me will live in peace, untroubled by fear of harm.

Proverbs 29:25
Fearing people is a dangerous trap, but trusting the Lord means safety.

Hebrews 13:6
So we can say with confidence, "The Lord is my helper, so I will have no fear. What can mere people do to me?"

When you feel like no one cares

Job 28:24
For he looks throughout the whole earth and sees everything under the heavens.

Job 31:4
Doesn't he see everything I do and every step I take?

Job 34:21
For God watches how people live; he sees everything they do.

Psalm 23:1-3
The Lord is my shepherd; I have all that I need. He lets me rest in green meadows; he leads me beside peaceful streams. He renews my strength. He guides me along right paths, bringing honor to his name.

Psalm 34:14-15
Turn away from evil and do good. Search for peace, and work to maintain it. The eyes of the Lord watch over those who do right; his ears are open to their cries for help.

Psalm 121:2-3
My help comes from the Lord, who made heaven and earth! He will not let you stumble; the one who watches over you will not slumber.

Song of Solomon 2:14
My dove is hiding behind the rocks, behind an outcrop on the cliff. Let me see your face; let me hear your voice.
For your voice is pleasant, and your face is lovely.

Matthew 6:25-34
"That is why I tell you not to worry about everyday life—whether you have enough food and drink, or enough clothes to wear. Isn't life more than food, and your body more than clothing? Look at the birds. They don't plant or harvest or store food in barns, for your heavenly Father feeds them. And aren't you far more valuable to him than they are? Can all your worries add a single moment to your life?

"And why worry about your clothing? Look at the lilies of the field and how they grow. They don't work or make their clothing, yet Solomon in all his glory was not dressed as beautifully as they are. And if God cares so wonderfully for wildflowers that are here today and thrown into the fire tomorrow, he will certainly care for you. Why do you have so little faith?

"So don't worry about these things, saying, 'What will we eat? What will we drink? What will we wear?' These things dominate the thoughts of unbelievers, but your heavenly Father already knows all your needs. Seek the Kingdom of God above all else, and live righteously, and he will give you everything you need.
"So don't worry about tomorrow, for tomorrow will bring its own worries. Today's trouble is enough for today."

Luke 11:8
"But I tell you this—though he won't do it for friendship's sake, if you keep knocking long enough, he will get up and give you whatever you need because of your shameless persistence."

Luke 22:31-32
"Simon, Simon, Satan has asked to sift each of you like wheat. But I have pleaded in prayer for you, Simon, that your faith should not fail. So when you have repented and turned to me again, strengthen your brothers."

1 Peter 5:6-7, 10
So humble yourselves under the mighty power of God, and at the right time he will lift you up in honor. Give all your worries and cares to God, for he cares about you . . . In his kindness God called you to share in his eternal glory by means of Christ Jesus. So after you have suffered a little while, he will restore, support, and strengthen you, and he will place you on a firm foundation.

When you don't know what to do

Proverbs 4:7
Getting wisdom is the wisest thing you can do! And whatever else you do, develop good judgment.

Psalm 16:11
You will show me the way of life, granting me the joy of your presence and the pleasures of living with you forever.

Psalm 19:7-13
The instructions of the Lord are perfect, reviving the soul. The decrees of
the Lord are trustworthy, making wise the simple. The commandments of
the Lord are right, bringing joy to the heart. The commands of the Lord
are clear, giving insight for living. Reverence for the Lord is pure, lasting
forever. The laws of the Lord are true; each one is fair. They are more
desirable than gold, even the finest gold. They are sweeter than honey,
even honey dripping from the comb. They are a warning to your servant, a
great reward for those who obey them. How can I know all the sins lurking
in my heart? Cleanse me from these hidden faults. Keep your servant from
deliberate sins! Don't let them control me. Then I will be free of guilt and
innocent of great sin.

Proverbs 15:32-33
If you reject discipline, you only harm yourself; but if you listen to correc-
tion, you grow in understanding. Fear of the Lord teaches wisdom; humility precedes honor.

Proverbs 19:21
You can make many plans, but the Lord's purpose will prevail.

Proverbs 16:9
We can make our plans, but the Lord determines our steps.

Isaiah 30:18-26
So the Lord must wait for you to come to him so he can show you his
love and compassion. For the Lord is a faithful God. Blessed are those
who wait for his help. O people of Zion, who live in Jerusalem, you will
weep no more. He will be gracious if you ask for help. He will surely
respond to the sound of your cries. Though the Lord gave you adver-
sity for food and suffering for drink, he will still be with you to teach
you. You will see your teacher with your own eyes. Your own ears will
hear him. Right behind you a voice will say, "This is the way you should
go," whether to the right or to the left. Then you will destroy all your
silver idols and your precious gold images. You will throw them out like
filthy rags, saying to them, "Good riddance!" Then the Lord will bless
you with rain at planting time. There will be wonderful harvests and
plenty of pastureland for your livestock. The oxen and donkeys that till

the ground will eat good grain, its chaff blown away by the wind. In that day, when your enemies are slaughtered and the towers fall, there will be streams of water flowing down every mountain and hill. The moon will be as bright as the sun, and the sun will be seven times brighter—like the light of seven days in one! So it will be when the Lord begins to heal his people and cure the wounds he gave them.

1 Corinthians 6:19-20
Don't you realize that your body is the temple of the Holy Spirit, who lives in you and was given to you by God? You do not belong to yourself, for God bought you with a high price. So you must honor God with your body.

When you don't know God's promises for your life

Psalm 20:4-8
May he grant your heart's desires and make all your plans succeed. May we shout for joy when we hear of your victory and raise a victory banner in the name of our God. May the Lord answer all your prayers. Now I know that the Lord rescues his anointed king. He will answer him from his holy heaven and rescue him by his great power. Some nations boast of their chariots and horses, but we boast in the name of the Lord our God. Those nations will fall down and collapse, but we will rise up and stand firm.

Psalm 32:8
The Lord says, "I will guide you along the best pathway for your life. I will advise you and watch over you."

Proverbs 10:22
The blessing of the Lord makes a person rich, and he adds no sorrow with it.

Isaiah 32:15-20
Until at last the Spirit is poured out on us from heaven. Then the wilderness will become a fertile field, and the fertile field will yield bountiful crops. Justice will rule in the wilderness and righteousness in the fertile

field. And this righteousness will bring peace. Yes, it will bring quietness and confidence forever. My people will live in safety, quietly at home. They will be at rest. Even if the forest should be destroyed and the city torn down, the Lord will greatly bless his people. Wherever they plant seed, bountiful crops will spring up. Their cattle and donkeys will graze freely.

Isaiah 41:9-16
I have called you back from the ends of the earth, saying, "You are my servant." For I have chosen you and will not throw you away. Don't be afraid, for I am with you. Don't be discouraged, for I am your God. I will strengthen you and help you. I will hold you up with my victorious right hand. See, all your angry enemies lie there, confused and humiliated. Anyone who opposes you will die and come to nothing. You will look in vain for those who tried to conquer you. Those who attack you will come to nothing. For I hold you by your right hand—I, the Lord your God. And I say to you, "Don't be afraid. I am here to help you. Though you are a lowly worm, O Jacob, don't be afraid, people of Israel, for I will help you. I am the Lord, your Redeemer. I am the Holy One of Israel." You will be a new threshing instrument with many sharp teeth. You will tear your enemies apart, making chaff of mountains. You will toss them into the air, and the wind will blow them all away; a whirlwind will scatter them. Then you will rejoice in the Lord. You will glory in the Holy One of Israel.

Isaiah 54:2-3
Enlarge your house; build an addition. Spread out your home, and spare no expense! For you will soon be bursting at the seams. Your descendants will occupy other nations and resettle the ruined cities.

Isaiah 55:3
Come to me with your ears wide open. Listen, and you will find life. I will make an everlasting covenant with you. I will give you all the unfailing love I promised to David.

Jeremiah 29:11
"For I know the plans I have for you," says the Lord. "They are plans for good and not for disaster, to give you a future and a hope."

Daniel 6:3, 22-23, 27
Daniel soon proved himself more capable than all the other administrators and high officers. Because of Daniel's great ability, the king made plans to place him over the entire empire . . . "My God sent his angel to shut the lions' mouths so that they would not hurt me, for I have been found innocent in his sight. And I have not wronged you, Your Majesty." The king was overjoyed and ordered that Daniel be lifted from the den. Not a scratch was found on him, for he had trusted in his God . . . "He rescues and saves his people; he performs miraculous signs and wonders in the heavens and on earth. He has rescued Daniel from the power of the lions."

Habakkuk 2:3
This vision is for a future time. It describes the end, and it will be fulfilled. If it seems slow in coming, wait patiently, for it will surely take place. It will not be delayed.

Joel 2:25-27
The Lord says, "I will give you back what you lost to the swarming locusts, the hopping locusts, the stripping locusts, and the cutting locusts. It was I who sent this great destroying army against you. Once again you will have all the food you want, and you will praise the Lord your God, who does these miracles for you. Never again will my people be disgraced. Then you will know that I am among my people Israel, that I am the Lord your God, and there is no other. Never again will my people be disgraced."

1 Corinthians 2:9
That is what the Scriptures mean when they say, "No eye has seen, no ear has heard, and no mind has imagined what God has prepared for those who love him."

2 Corinthians 9:8
And God will generously provide all you need. Then you will always have everything you need and plenty left over to share with others.

James 5:11
We give great honor to those who endure under suffering. For instance, you know about Job, a man of great endurance. You can see how the Lord was kind to him at the end, for the Lord is full of tenderness and mercy.

When you feel like no one understands

Psalm 33:13-15
The Lord looks down from heaven and sees the whole human race. From his throne he observes all who live on the earth. He made their hearts, so he understands everything they do.

When you have trouble forgiving those who hurt you

Psalm 37:1-7
Don't worry about the wicked or envy those who do wrong. For like grass, they soon fade away. Like spring flowers, they soon wither. Trust in the Lord and do good. Then you will live safely in the land and prosper. Take delight in the Lord, and he will give you your heart's desires. Commit everything you do to the Lord. Trust him, and he will help you. He will make your innocence radiate like the dawn, and the justice of your cause will shine like the noonday sun. Be still in the presence of the Lord, and wait patiently for him to act. Don't worry about evil people who prosper or fret about their wicked schemes.

Psalm 60:11-12
Oh, please help us against our enemies, for all human help is useless. With God's help we will do mighty things, for he will trample down our foes.

Hebrews 4:13
Nothing in all creation is hidden from God. Everything is naked and exposed before his eyes, and he is the one to whom we are accountable.

When you've lost hope

Psalm 43:5
Why am I discouraged? Why is my heart so sad? I will put my hope in God! I will praise him again—my Savior and my God!

Romans 8:28
And we know that God causes everything to work together for the good of those who love God and are called according to his purpose for them.

1 Corinthians 15:58
So, my dear brothers and sisters, be strong and immovable. Always work enthusiastically for the Lord, for you know that nothing you do for the Lord is ever useless.

2 Corinthians 1:4
He comforts us in all our troubles so that we can comfort others. When they are troubled, we will be able to give them the same comfort God has given us.

Galatians 6:8-9
Those who live only to satisfy their own sinful nature will harvest decay and death from that sinful nature. But those who live to please the Spirit will harvest everlasting life from the Spirit. So let's not get tired of doing what is good. At just the right time we will reap a harvest of blessing if we don't give up.

Hebrews 10:35-36
So do not throw away this confident trust in the Lord. Remember the great reward it brings you! Patient endurance is what you need now, so that you will continue to do God's will. Then you will receive all that he has promised.

James 1:2-4
Dear brothers and sisters, when troubles of any kind come your way, consider it an opportunity for great joy. For you know that when your faith is tested, your endurance has a chance to grow. So let it grow, for when your endurance is fully developed, you will be perfect and complete, needing nothing.
Revelation 3:8
I know all the things you do, and I have opened a door for you that no one can close. You have little strength, yet you obeyed my word and did not deny me.

When you need God's forgiveness

Psalm 51:7, 10
Purify me from my sins, and I will be clean; wash me, and I will be whiter than snow . . . Create in me a clean heart, O God. Renew a loyal spirit within me.

Isaiah 1:18
"Come now, let's settle this," says the Lord. "Though your sins are like scarlet, I will make them as white as snow. Though they are red like crimson, I will make them as white as wool."

Jeremiah 32:19
You have all wisdom and do great and mighty miracles. You see the conduct of all people, and you give them what they deserve.

Hosea 2:5-8, 14-20
"Their mother is a shameless prostitute and became pregnant in a shameful way. She said, 'I'll run after other lovers and sell myself to them for food and water, for clothing of wool and linen, and for olive oil and drinks.'
"For this reason I will fence her in with thornbushes. I will block her path with a wall to make her lose her way. When she runs after her lovers, she won't be able to catch them. She will search for them but not find them. Then she will think, 'I might as well return to my husband, for I was better off with him than I am now.' She doesn't realize it was I who gave her everything she has—the grain, the new wine, the olive oil; I even gave her silver and gold. But she gave all my gifts to Baal . . .
"But then I will win her back once again. I will lead her into the desert and speak tenderly to her there. I will return her vineyards to her and transform the Valley of Trouble into a gateway of hope. She will give herself to me there, as she did long ago when she was young, when I freed her from her captivity in Egypt. When that day comes," says the Lord, "you will call me 'my husband' instead of 'my master.' O Israel, I will wipe the many names of Baal from your lips, and you will never mention them again. On that day I will make a covenant with all the wild animals and the birds of the sky and the animals that scurry along the ground so they will not harm you. I will remove all weapons of war from the land, all swords and bows, so you can live unafraid in peace and safety. I will make you my wife forever, showing you righteousness and justice, unfailing love and compassion. I will be faithful to you and make you mine, and you will finally know me as the Lord."

When you have a deep inner longing that no one can fill

Psalm 63:1-11
O God, you are my God; I earnestly search for you. My soul thirsts for
you; my whole body longs for you in this parched and weary land where
there is no water. I have seen you in your sanctuary and gazed upon your
power and glory. Your unfailing love is better than life itself; how I praise
you! I will praise you as long as I live, lifting up my hands to you in prayer.
You satisfy me more than the richest feast. I will praise you with songs
of joy. I lie awake thinking of you, meditating on you through the night.
Because you are my helper, I sing for joy in the shadow of your wings. I
cling to you; your strong right hand holds me securely. But those plotting
to destroy me will come to ruin. They will go down into the depths of the
earth. They will die by the sword and become the food of jackals. But the
king will rejoice in God. All who swear to tell the truth will praise him,
while liars will be silenced.

Psalm 73:25-26
Whom have I in heaven but you? I desire you more than anything on
earth. My health may fail, and my spirit may grow weak, but God remains
the strength of my heart; he is mine forever.

When you wonder if God can heal you

Psalm 84:4-7
What joy for those who can live in your house, always singing your praises.
What joy for those whose strength comes from the Lord, who have set their
minds on a pilgrimage to Jerusalem. When they walk through the Valley
of Weeping, it will become a place of refreshing springs. The autumn rains
will clothe it with blessings. They will continue to grow stronger, and each
of them will appear before God in Jerusalem.

Psalm 118:22-24
The stone that the builders rejected has now become the cornerstone. This
is the Lord's doing, and it is wonderful to see. This is the day the Lord has
made. We will rejoice and be glad in it.

Psalm 147:3
He heals the brokenhearted and bandages their wounds.

Luke 8:48
"Daughter," he said to her, "your faith has made you well. Go in peace."

Acts 3:5-8
The lame man looked at them eagerly, expecting some money. But Peter said, "I don't have any silver or gold for you. But I'll give you what I have. In the name of Jesus Christ the Nazarene, get up and walk!" Then Peter took the lame man by the right hand and helped him up. And as he did, the man's feet and ankles were instantly healed and strengthened. He jumped up, stood on his feet, and began to walk! Then, walking, leaping, and praising God, he went into the Temple with them.

Revelation 7:17
For the Lamb on the throne will be their Shepherd. He will lead them to springs of life-giving water. And God will wipe every tear from their eyes.

When you wonder if you can change

Proverbs 25:28
A person without self-control is like a city with broken-down walls.

Proverbs 31:10
Who can find a virtuous and capable wife? She is more precious than rubies.

Ecclesiastes 3:1-4
For everything there is a season, a time for every activity under heaven. A time to be born and a time to die. A time to plant and a time to harvest. A time to kill and a time to heal. A time to tear down and a time to build up. A time to cry and a time to laugh. A time to grieve and a time to dance.

Jeremiah 17:9
The human heart is the most deceitful of all things, and desperately wicked. Who really knows how bad it is?

Luke 17:32-33
"Remember what happened to Lot's wife! If you cling to your life, you will lose it, and if you let your life go, you will save it."

Romans 6:6
We know that our old sinful selves were crucified with Christ so that sin might lose its power in our lives. We are no longer slaves to sin.

Romans 7:21–8:2
I have discovered this principle of life—that when I want to do what is right, I inevitably do what is wrong. I love God's law with all my heart. But there is another power within me that is at war with my mind. This power makes me a slave to the sin that is still within me. Oh, what a miserable person I am! Who will free me from this life that is dominated by sin and death? Thank God! The answer is in Jesus Christ our Lord. So you see how it is: In my mind I really want to obey God's law, but because of my sinful nature I am a slave to sin. So now there is no condemnation for those who belong to Christ Jesus. And because you belong to him, the power of the life-giving Spirit has freed you from the power of sin that leads to death.

Romans 12:2
Don't copy the behavior and customs of this world, but let God transform you into a new person by changing the way you think. Then you will learn to know God's will for you, which is good and pleasing and perfect.

1 Corinthians 13:11
When I was a child, I spoke and thought and reasoned as a child. But when I grew up, I put away childish things.

2 Corinthians 5:17
This means that anyone who belongs to Christ has become a new person. The old life is gone; a new life has begun!

2 Corinthians 10:4-5
We use God's mighty weapons, not worldly weapons, to knock down the strongholds of human reasoning and to destroy false arguments. We destroy every proud obstacle that keeps people from knowing God. We capture their rebellious thoughts and teach them to obey Christ.

2 Corinthians 12:9-10
Each time he said, "My grace is all you need. My power works best in weakness." So now I am glad to boast about my weaknesses, so that the power of Christ can work through me. That's why I take pleasure in my weaknesses, and in the insults, hardships, persecutions, and troubles that I suffer for Christ. For when I am weak, then I am strong.

Philippians 1:6
And I am certain that God, who began the good work within you, will continue his work until it is finally finished on the day when Christ Jesus returns.

Philippians 3:13-14
No, dear brothers and sisters, I have not achieved it, but I focus on this one thing: Forgetting the past and looking forward to what lies ahead, I press on to reach the end of the race and receive the heavenly prize for which God, through Christ Jesus, is calling us.

Colossians 3:10, 12-13
Put on your new nature, and be renewed as you learn to know your Creator and become like him . . . Since God chose you to be the holy people he loves, you must clothe yourselves with tenderhearted mercy, kindness, humility, gentleness, and patience. Make allowance for each other's faults, and forgive anyone who offends you. Remember, the Lord forgave you, so you must forgive others.

Hebrews 12:1-2
Therefore, since we are surrounded by such a huge crowd of witnesses to the life of faith, let us strip off every weight that slows us down, especially the sin that so easily trips us up. And let us run with endurance the race God has set before us. We do this by keeping our eyes on Jesus, the champion who initiates and perfects our faith. Because of the joy awaiting him, he endured the cross, disregarding its shame. Now he is seated in the place of honor beside God's throne.

When you don't think God can use you

Isaiah 61:1
The Spirit of the Sovereign Lord is upon me, for the Lord has anointed me to bring good news to the poor. He has sent me to comfort the brokenhearted and to proclaim that captives will be released and prisoners will be freed.

Jeremiah 1:4-5
The Lord gave me this message: "I knew you before I formed you in your mother's womb. Before you were born I set you apart and appointed you as my prophet to the nations."

Acts 1:8
"But you will receive power when the Holy Spirit comes upon you. And you will be my witnesses, telling people about me everywhere—in Jerusalem, throughout Judea, in Samaria, and to the ends of the earth."

Ephesians 3:7-8
By God's grace and mighty power, I have been given the privilege of serving him by spreading this Good News. Though I am the least deserving of all God's people, he graciously gave me the privilege of telling the Gentiles about the endless treasures available to them in Christ.

When you don't feel loved

John 3:16
"For this is how God loved the world: He gave his one and only Son, so that everyone who believes in him will not perish but have eternal life."

John 14:18, 27, 30
"No, I will not abandon you as orphans—I will come to you . . . I am leaving you with a gift—peace of mind and heart. And the peace I give is a gift the world cannot give. So don't be troubled or afraid . . . I don't have much more time to talk to you, because the ruler of this world approaches. He has no power over me."

Romans 5:8
But God showed his great love for us by sending Christ to die for us while we were still sinners.

1 John 4:9-10
God showed how much he loved us by sending his one and only Son into the world so that we might have eternal life through him. This is real love—not that we loved God, but that he loved us and sent his Son as a sacrifice to take away our sins.

Sermons

Anointed Fire Ministries (www.anointedfire.com)
Frustration of Waiting for a Mate

Pastor Keith Battle (www.zionlandover.com)
The Blessing of Getting Caught
Let Him Finish
But You
Understanding and Overcoming Addictions
Purpose, part 2 (6/15/2014)
Loneliness, parts 1 and 2
Purpose, part 12: The Deal Breaker
What I Learned in the Turns
Side Chickology
The Power of Punctuation
Nuggets for Your Journey

Bishop T.D. Jakes (www.thepottershouse.org)
Nothing That You've Been Through Will Be Wasted
Destiny Steps
Destiny Has Two Hands
Destiny Steps: Focus
Destiny Steps: Distinctively Similar
Destiny Steps: Just Do It
Destiny Steps: Process to Progress
5 Stages of Recovery

Fit for the Fight
Faith Is an Equalizer
You're the Man

Pastor James Marshall (www.zionlandover.com)
Message to Singles
You Gotta Get Low

Bishop Rudolph McKissick Jr (www.thebethelexperience.com)
Stuck in a Rut

Joyce Meyer (www.joycemeyer.org)
The Cure for the Insecure
An Attitude of Trust and Patience

Pastor Larry Paige (www.zionlandover.com)
Get Over It (7/29/2014)

Pastor Toure Roberts (www.onechurchla.org)
5 Keys to Identifying Your Soul Mate

Sarah Jakes Roberts (www.sarahjakesroberts.com)
Lost and Found webisodes

Dr. Jasmine Sculark (www.iamdrjazz.org)
It's Not about the Water

Songs

Yolanda Adams
Still I Rise
That Name

India Arie
A Beautiful Day
This Too Shall Pass

Private Party
I Am Light
There's Hope

Arkansas Gospel Mass Choir
I Lift My Hands

Myron Butler
Speak

Jekalyn Carr
Greater Is Coming

Kelly Clarkson
Stronger (What Doesn't Kill You)

Tasha Cobbs
Smile
Break Every Chain

Patrick Dopson
Keep Me

Fantasia
Doing Me
Lose to Win

Lawrence Flowers & Intercession
Job Experience

James Fortune & FIYA
The Curse Is Broken
Empty Me

Fred Hammond
I Will Trust
Your Steps Are Ordered

Hillsong United
All I Need Is You

Israel Houghton
Moving Forward

Israel and New Breed
To Worship You

John P. Kee
The Anointing

Tori Kelly
Dear No One

Tamela Mann
I Can Only Imagine

Vashawn Mitchell
Turning Around for Me

Chante Moore
Jesus, I Want You

Smokie Norful
No Greater Love

Jill Scott
Golden
Kierra Sheard
Free

The Tri-City Singers
Love the Hurt Away

Bishop Larry Trotter & Sweet Holy Spirit
It's Only a Test

Kim Walker
How He Loves Us

Ted Winn
God Believes in You

Movies

Facing the Giants
The Gabby Douglas Story
Things Never Said
This Is Our Time
30 for 30: You Don't Know Bo – The Legend of Bo Jackson

Books

Vicki Courtney
Move On

Tony Evans
30 Days to Overcoming Emotional Strongholds

Sarah Jakes Roberts
Lost & Found

Bishop T.D. Jakes
Daddy Loves His Girls

Stephanie Perry Moore
A Lova' Like No Otha'

Francine Rivers
Redeeming Love

David Steele
Conscious Dating

Iyanla Vanzant
Forgiveness
Peace from Broken Pieces

Holly Virden and Michelle McKinney Hammond
If Singleness Is a Gift, What's The Return Policy?

Charles Whitfield
A Gift to Myself: A Personal Workbook and Guide to "Healing the Child Within"

H. Norman Wright
Healing for the Father Wound

William P. Young
The Shack

About the Author

Shavon Carter is The "YOU" Relationship Coach, as well as an author, speaker, and liturgical dancer, with a passion for empowering women to fulfill their life's purpose. She is the founder of Walking in Wholeness, LLC, through which she helps women from all backgrounds walk in their awesomeness. She is also the co-founder of Living4Today Inspirations, Inc., through which she writes daily inspirations filled with Godly revelation and wisdom to uplift the soul and rejuvenate the spirit. In December 2011, she published her first book, *Living For Today: Inspirations for the Soul*, to encourage those on the verge of giving up hope in different areas of their lives.

Shavon is a native of Jacksonville, Florida, but currently resides in Bowie, Maryland. She graduated from Florida A&M University in 2001 with a bachelor's degree in accounting. In 2004, she obtained a Master's in Business Administration from the University of Phoenix–Northern Virginia campus. She is employed with the Department of Defense as an Audit Director.

Shavon is a member of Zion Church, a non-denominational ministry in Landover, Maryland, where Keith Battle is the senior pastor.

www.ingramcontent.com/pod-product-compliance
Lightning Source LLC
LaVergne TN
LVHW021455080426
835509LV00018B/2297